FACING
the
FUTURE
without
FEAR

FACING *the* FUTURE *without* FEAR

Prescriptions for Courageous Living in the New Millennium

LLOYD JOHN OGILVIE
CHAPLAIN OF THE U.S. SENATE

SERVANT PUBLICATIONS
ANN ARBOR, MICHIGAN

Vine Books is an imprint of Servant Publications especially designed to serve evangelical
Christians.

Published by Servant Publications
P.O. Box 8617
Ann Arbor, Michigan 48107

Cover Design: Alan Furst, Inc., Minneapolis, Minn.
Cover Photograph: Corbis, Used by Permission

01 02 03 04   10 9 8 7 6 5 4 3 2

Printed in the United States of America
ISBN 1-56955-326-2

To Senator Max Cleland
who exemplifies that God's perfect love casts out fear.

CONTENTS

Preface

September 11, 2001, began like most other days for me: early morning Bible reading and prayer; a walk around the Capitol, praying for the senators; then back home for breakfast. I live on the Hill just ten minutes from the Capitol, so I calculated the time I would need in order to be on the Senate floor to give the opening prayer at 10:00 A.M.

I walked through the living room on my way out. The television was focused on the World Trade Center in New York City. At that very moment I saw an American Airlines plane fly into one of the towers. "This must be an old movie!" I exclaimed. Then the newscaster's voice cried out, "A commercial jet has just flown into one of the towers of the World Trade Center!" Inside I knew that no plane would be that far off course. This had to be a terrorist attack!

I ran out of the house and down Constitution Avenue to the Capitol. A policeman at the entrance confirmed my worst assumption: America was being attacked. It seemed as if the elevator took forever to reach the third floor of the Capitol and my office, which looks out over the Mall and the Washington Monument. When I reached the office, my assistant told me a second plane had crashed into the other World Trade Tower. As the minutes ticked by leading up to the 10:00 Senate opening, I started to rewrite my prayer. As I dictated it to my assistant at her computer, I looked out the window and, suddenly, I saw gigantic clouds of black smoke rising from the Pentagon. It, too, had been hit by a commercial jet turned into a weapon of destruction.

At that moment, a policeman pounded on the door. "Evacuate the Capitol! Evacuate the Capitol!" he shouted. I dropped everything and joined my staff in running down the steps, out of the building, and onto the front lawn on the east side of the Capitol. Hundreds of Senate and House of Representatives staff, along with members of the media, were milling about, talking excitedly, with panicked looks on their faces. Rumors of a fourth plane heading for the Capitol Building intensified the fear.

I raised my hand and shouted, "Everyone gather around me. We need to pray!" The anxiety was palpable in the crowd that huddled together for prayer. Many in the large crowd cried out, "Lord, help us!" as I prayed.

As I finished, police officers swarmed onto the lawn, shouting, "Move away from the building!" One confided to us that another plane was indeed headed for the Capitol. I'll never forget the frenzy of the crowd running away from the Capitol. Fear gripped them. Some raced for child-care centers to get their children; others tried to retrieve their cars and head for home; still others walked or ran fearfully, trying to avoid some unknown catastrophe.

The leaders of the Senate were whisked away to secret, safe places. The rest of the senators were sequestered in the Capitol Police Headquarters Building, where they remained throughout the day, watching on television the further events of the terrorist attack. There was silence when it was announced that the fourth plane, apparently headed for Washington, had crashed in Pennsylvania. The strong supposition was that it had been aimed at the Capitol Building. When its flight pattern was announced, I realized that had it made it to its final destination, it would have come up over the Washington Mall and right into the window of my third-floor office!

All through the day we watched the oft-repeated footage of the collapse of the Trade Center Towers and the grim announcements of the growing list of fatalities and those seriously wounded. Tension mounted in the Police Building as intelligence was shared about the perpetrators of this war on the United States.

At the end of the afternoon, the senators huddled together in a "safe room" of the Police Building for a conference call with the Senate majority and minority leaders. They faced the crisis and made plans for how the Senate would handle the threatening circumstances. They also decided that the Senate should join with the House of Representatives for a prayer meeting in the Rotunda of the Capitol the following evening. The chaplains of the House and Senate were asked to plan the service.

It was a profoundly moving service, with the members and officers of both houses of Congress and their spouses gathered in a solemn assembly in the Rotunda. The Marine Corps Band played, the colors were posted, and the Pledge of Allegiance was recited with patriotic intensity. I opened the prayer service with the following call to prayer and invocation:

We come together to affirm our faith in God, Sovereign of this nation and Lord of our lives. We come with heavy hearts filled with profound grief for our fellow Americans who perished in the terrorist attack on the World Trade Center and the Pentagon.

With love and care, we reach out to the families and loved ones and gather in this historic Rotunda of our nation's Capitol to pray for them, asking God to comfort them and give them courage. It is as fellow Americans that we affirm our oneness of trust in God and patriotism to our beloved nation.

Our help is in the name of the Lord, who made heaven and earth. Let us pray.

Gracious God, Faithful Father, Loving Lord. You have promised to keep us in perfect peace when our minds are stayed on You. Do for us what we cannot do for ourselves. Keep our minds on You! Lift up our hearts! Infuse our thinking with Your peace, Your shalom, the peace that passes understanding, the peace that places a balm of healing on our raw nerves, the peace that makes us secure in Your everlasting arms. You alone can heal the immense grief of our nation following yesterday's tragedy and loss.

You alone are the source of comfort for the immense pain, loneliness, and anguish that the families of the victims of yesterday's terrorist attacks have suffered and will endure. Blessed God, be the unseen but powerful presence in their homes, the strength to their spouses, the eternal Father to fatherless children, a friend to those whose friends have perished in violent death. Mend their broken hearts and fill them with courage.

Thank You for the memory of those gallant police officers and firefighters who gave their lives to protect others. May we never forget their heroism and commitment. As members and officers of the Senate and House of Representatives of Congress, we intercede for Your care of their families; strengthen them and give them an assurance of Your presence. May they know that death came as no conqueror in the end; You met them as their eternal friend. Now in this memorial service, fill our hearts with hope and an assurance that death is not an ending but a transition in eternal life. You are our Lord and Savior. Amen.

Members of both the House of Representatives and the Senate spoke, and the service was closed in a very powerful way by the House chaplain, Father Dan Coughlin.

On Friday, while the senators joined President Bush for a memorial service at the National Cathedral, I felt led to hold a prayer vigil for Senate staff. I arranged for a room to accommodate three hundred, and more than six hundred showed up! They filled the room, many standing crowded together, and others sitting on the floor. When my friend Rabbi Levi Shemtov arrived with more than a hundred more, people gave up their chairs and welcomed the contingent with applause. A palpable spirit of unity was evident as the vigil progressed with prayers from the staffers and concluded with the singing of "God Bless America" as we held hands.

The following week, I accompanied the senators to "ground zero," where the Trade Center Towers had stood. As I looked at the ghastly heap of wreckage, filled with bodies of victims, I exclaimed to myself, "That looks like the gates of hell!" Instantly, Jesus' words, set to the music of a great anthem, thundered through my mind: "The gates of hell shall not prevail!"

Talking to the gallant firefighters moved me deeply. As I hugged and encouraged them, I thought of those from their ranks who had died while trying to save others, particularly those who had willingly entered the Towers to help others, knowing they might not survive. Heroes and heroines indeed!

While the Senate family reeled with the impact of September 11, and tried to deal with the fear of further attacks, we were hit with anthrax anxiety. Letters containing anthrax resulted in the testing of several thousand people. The latent fear of sickness and death was unleashed in many. My counseling ministry increased, and small groups were formed to help the Senate staff deal with the panic of bio-terrorism. The contents of this book were used as a guide for Bible study and discussion groups.

Courage results from convictions that cannot be compromised. I published the following list of convictions in an effort to help people think clearly and live courageously:

- God does not send suffering, cause crises, or try us with tragedies. We dismiss the false question: Where was God in the midst of the terrorist attack on September 11? He was with us, suffering with us, giving us courage and hope.
- God created humankind to know, love, and serve Him. We reverently reflect on what must have been His most crucial decision to give us freedom of will, knowing that there can be no response of love from us to Him without choice, but also knowing that we would abuse and misuse our freedom.
- There is an objective force of evil in the world that often is expressed through people, movements, and nations. Heinous acts happen. God is not dissuaded. He shares the suffering of those who are victims of evil, and in ways we could not imagine, brings good out of evil.
- Our greatest enemy is death. And yet, God has defeated the power of death. In the midst of our anguish over those lost in the September 11 tragedies, we are reminded of the shortness of time and the length of eternity.
- We are called to be communicators of hope, love, and strength to those who suffer in the grim aftermath of terrorism. "Though the wrong seems oft so strong, God is the ruler yet!"

- We have been called to be a nation under God with a unique role in the family of nations. We need to maintain the greatness of our nation as declared in our Constitution and dramatized in our history. Now is the time for a fresh commitment to patriotism for all of us, so that we may remain strong and be examples of freedom to the world.

Now my prayer is that the twelve prescriptions for facing the future without fear that are explained in this book will help you deal with your own fears. America will never be the same again. We are at war with a treacherous, illusive enemy. We are going to win, but in the meantime, here's a strategy for overcoming fear, rather than being overwhelmed by it.

Lloyd J. Ogilvie

PROBING THE RAW NERVE

Georgia Senator Max Cleland steered his wheelchair into the room—a private area near the Senate chamber where I have the privilege of leading a Bible study for senators each Thursday noon. Max was not his usual jovial self. His face revealed anxiety and lack of sound sleep.

Max lost both legs and his right hand when a grenade accidentally exploded on a hilltop in Vietnam thirty-one years ago. Since then he has spent many a sleepless night haunted by fearsome memories from the accident and fearful thoughts about making it through the challenges of the next day. The syndrome of repetitive fear had finally taken its toll.

After my Bible study message and discussion, the senators usually share needs and concerns and pray for each other. One of the senators said, "Max, how can we pray for you?" Max related what had been happening to him. The group of senators responded by gathering around him, asking for healing of memories and renewed strength.

What happened a few days later was a direct answer to the senators' prayers.

Max appeared on a television program during which he was asked to tell about his accident. He recalled a valley called Khe Sanh in Vietnam. It was a dangerous area just fourteen miles from the demilitarized zone. About five thousand American marines were trapped in the valley with more than twenty thousand North Vietnamese troops in the surrounding hills. The only way to reach the American troops was by helicopter. A large-scale, joint army-marine effort was mounted.

Twenty-five-year-old Captain Max Cleland flew to a hill east of Khe Sanh. He jumped off the helicopter, followed by the men under his command. When they were clear of the chopper blades, they watched the helicopter lift into the air. That's when the horror and confusion began. Max noticed a hand grenade on the ground before him. "I went toward it," he said. "It wasn't a heroic act. I just thought it was mine." What he didn't know was that the grenade pin had become dislodged. The grenade exploded, throwing Max backward. When the smoke cleared, his right hand and most of his right leg were gone and his left leg was a smoldering bloody mass of flesh.

Max explained, "The blast jammed my eyeballs into my skull, temporarily blinding me, pinning my cheeks and jaw muscles to the bones of my face. My ears rang with deafening reverberation, as if I were standing in an echo chamber."

That was April 8, 1968, and since that day Max has lived with the uncertainty and fear that he was to blame—that his carelessness in dropping the grenade had caused his own wounds.

A few days after the television interview, David Lloyd, a former marine who had seen the program, called the senator. Lloyd helped Max refresh his memory. Lloyd had been on that same hill in Vietnam back in 1968. After the explosion, he wrapped a tourniquet around Max's thigh. Then he tended to another soldier covered with blood. This was the young man's first day in combat. He cried out to Lloyd, "It was my grenade! It was my grenade!" Out of inexperience the soldier had loosened the pins on his grenades to make them easier to activate in combat and then dropped one of them. It had not been Max's grenade after all!

Hearing these words left Max feeling like he had been hit with "a second emotional grenade."

"After Dave told me this," he said, " I didn't get much sleep that next night, because it opened up all the old wounds, all the old thoughts that I had tried to lay aside to get on with my life. Can you imagine living with something like this ... living with the mystery, not the knowledge, but the mystery that somehow or another you might have screwed up somehow?"

Now the Lord has intervened to help Max know the truth and to lift the fear-impacted burden of self-incrimination and guilt.

The senator's face was radiant with joy when he returned to the Bible study the following Thursday. David Lloyd's revelation had brought a profound emotional healing into his life. The prayers of the senators' Bible study group had been answered.

You and I have fears that need to be healed too—plenty of them. In fact, fear has reached epidemic proportions in America today. It is contagious. We become infected by it and pass it on to others. Like a disease, fear saps our energy and robs us of joy in life.

Far from being the exclusive problem of the neurotic, fear cripples people everywhere and often pervades our families, even our churches. Even here in Washington, beneath the highly polished surface of powerful leaders, there's a lot of fear. During the past four years, I've had the privilege of serving as chaplain of the United States Senate and of coming to grips with the insidious power of fear. I've experienced it in myself, and I see it in others.

The joy of working with leaders and their staffs has led me to a reaffirmation of some basic prescriptions for living without the crippling power of fear.

I'll never forget being interviewed for a television talk show by a woman whose public image seemed to be a polished combination of Barbara Walters and Diane Sawyer. She projected a "Miss Put-Together" image of personal and professional competence. After introducing me, the woman asked, "What are you working on now?"

I told her I was writing a book on fear. With her encouragement, I explained that I had once asked my television and radio audience to write me about whatever fears were keeping them from living with freedom and joy. The responses, I told the television interviewer, had really helped me feel the pulse beat of fear in people today.

The woman picked up on my statement. I sensed more than the personal interest of a skilled interviewer. The look on her face betrayed her own battle with fear.

We got into one of the deepest conversations I've ever had during a live television interview. The woman seemed to lose all track of time as she pressed me to explain how to cope with fear. A scheduled five-minute interview went on for twenty-five minutes. Other guests had to be held over for the next day's broadcast.

After we went off the air, the director came into the studio. He was a bit upset. "Didn't you see me signaling you?" he asked her. "I didn't know how I was going to get you off the air. I almost pulled the plug on you two."

"Sorry!" she responded. "We were probing the raw nerve in people today. It just couldn't be rushed."

After the director and camera crew left, the woman confided, "I guess our conversation really pushed my button!" We sat in the studio for a long visit over coffee. Now off the air, she could be more personal, describing her own brand of fear. Though she was a success, she fought a gnawing insecurity about her future as a person and as a performer.

"It's the nights that are hard," she said. "I wake up at three o'clock wondering whether I can pull off another day's program. Will I fall flat on my face? I guess that's why I found the interview this morning so vital to me."

Here was a popular, admired performer who was filled with the same types of fears that I sense gnaw at nearly everyone these days. We had a deep conversation about how God could help her with her fear. I was surprised at how willing she was for me to pray for her before I left the studio.

Franklin Delano Roosevelt recognized the destructive power of fear when he said, "The only thing we have to fear is fear itself." That's a memorable statement. Yet fearing fear does not help us conquer it. If that were all it took, you and I would have defeated fear long ago!

Cheap advice and simplistic sermons don't help, either. We've all been told we shouldn't fear, just as if all we had to do was to decide we weren't going to be fearful anymore. So we feel guilty, thinking that we could get over our fear if we just tried harder. As a result, our fear increases.

To put it bluntly, we can't take fear. Fear takes us. And a good deal of the time we feel helpless in controlling it.

We question with British novelist Joseph Conrad, "How does one kill fear, I wonder? How do you shoot a specter through the heart, slash off its spectral head, take it by the spectral throat?"

That's what millions of people today want to know. What can we do with our fears?

WHERE DOES THE FEAR COME FROM?

We can begin by identifying them. It's important to realize that our fears come from four different but interconnected worlds.

Our Frightening Global World
Sometimes we blame our fears on the frightening world in which we live. Just reading the front page of any day's newspaper is enough to give us a bad case of the jitters. The possibility of nuclear annihilation, the virulence of cancer, the alarming spread of AIDS, the danger of terrorism and violence, the threat of global recession, the breakdown of moral integrity— these are only a few of the thousands of things that keep us agitated.

Many would echo A.E. Housman's sentiments:

> I, a stranger and afraid
> In a world I never made.

Our Private World
Not all our fears make the daily newspaper. Our private worlds—the family, workplace, neighborhood, even the church—include distressing situations and fear-producing encounters. We fear we will be misunderstood. We fear someone will take advantage of us. We fear we will not perform up to the standards we set for ourselves or others set for us. What is it for you?

Who or what in your immediate world causes you fear?

Our Personal World

Fear is not *primarily caused* by the world around us but comes from within us and then is attached to people and problems we face. Often what we quickly name as a fear in a particular situation is not what we really fear. Our outer fears are connected to much more profound internal fears.

Fear is nurtured and grown in a person's inner world of thought, emotion, memory, and imagination. Until our inner fears are overcome, we'll wage a losing battle with alarm over the world's problems and our immediate circumstances.

This inner world of fear has been a lifelong concern to me. As I've tried to deal with my own fears and help others battle theirs, I've usually found that surface fears are expanded and exaggerated by unresolved internal fears.

To explore this inner world, over the years I have asked people, "What fear inside you keeps you from living to the fullest?"

The thousands of responses I've received from the church I pastored in Hollywood, from my ministry to television and radio congregations across the country, and from men and women I now serve in Washington have been revealing. By breaking responses down into categories, I came up with a list of real troublemakers. The most disturbing fears included the fear caused by hurting memories, the fear of rejection, the fear of losing control, the fear of being inadequate, the fear of sickness and death, and the fear of the future.

An Even Deeper World of Fear

The more I've thought about these inner fears, the more convinced I have become that they are connected to an even deeper world inside all of us. This is the realm of our most private self, known only to us and to God. From there, in the core of our innermost souls, the taproot of fear sends out its shoots into our thoughts; the shoots wind themselves around people and circumstances in our immediate world, and then they blossom into a fearful reaction to the alarming problems in the world at large.

All our efforts to overcome fear on the other three levels will fail until we experience healing in the depth of our souls. It's there in the secret place of our spirits that we need to receive profound love, the only lasting antidote to fear. And only God can love us as much as we need to be loved. Not just once, but daily—hour by hour, moment by moment.

THE IDEA FOR THIS BOOK

From this need came the idea for this book: Wouldn't it be great to have prescriptions for living without fear—prescriptions that first address our deepest fears? Once we root out those fears, we can confront the fears in our personal world. After that we'd be able to face the fears in our interpersonal world and finally gain confidence to live with fearless freedom in the perplexing, broader world of our culture.

My hope is that you will consider all of the following prescriptions for living without fear. To act on them, I suggest you review them at the beginning of each day. As you internalize the principles laid out here, you will be better able to face potentially frightening pressures and problems. In a time of history dominated by fear, you and I can become part of a fearless minority. We can lead a counterculture campaign against our archenemy: fear.

To protect the privacy of my conversations and counseling, anecdotes and illustrations throughout the book use first names only, and fictitious ones at that.

With this background on the arenas of fear and with this challenge before us, we are ready to take the first step toward living without fear.

Chapter One

FEAR WHAT?

PRESCRIPTION 1:
Your fear is really loneliness for God.
Therefore, claim His promise never to leave nor forsake you.

Fear is loneliness for God. We were created to receive His love and love Him. And He has chosen and called us to live in an intimate relationship with Him. He is the Initiator of that relationship, constantly seeking us, pursuing us with relentless love.

Many of us all our lives have heard and read about God's grace, and yet we still battle with fear. Why is it so difficult for us to claim God's love?

THE SHORTEST SERMON ON RECORD

John Albrecht, an Episcopal priest in Lake Orion, Michigan, wanted to "reach" his congregation with the shortest sermon ever preached. He stepped behind his pulpit. After a long pause, he said, "Love!" Then he sat down. A long period of silence followed.

His proclamation was cited in *The Guinness Book of World Records.* Some of the members of Albrecht's church said it was his best sermon! It would be difficult to tie that record with a better word. Love says it all.

And yet simply saying the word *love* does not make it real. I'm sure that some people in the congregation that morning felt frustrated. Others probably felt guilt over their own lack of love for others and then perhaps unsettled about their lack of love for themselves. But if what I'm hearing from people today is representative, I think most of the congregation that day felt a deep surge of loneliness. My friend Tim used to respond that way to constant reminders of God's love.

Love? Whose love? God's? he used to wonder. *If God loves me, why do I have all this trouble? Where is He when I need Him? Is He really in control? Then why don't I sense His presence? Perhaps He's like most people—big promises and little performance.*

Tim has had lots of disappointments with people through the years. His dad left him and his mother when Tim was twelve—just when he needed a dad the most. Friends let him down. And the most shattering blow of all was when his wife left him. It was a long, lonely separation. And even though she's come back, Tim can't really believe she's home to stay.

ABANDONMENT

If I were to write the shortest chapter on a basic cause of fear, I would print one word: *abandonment.* And if I wanted to get extravagant with length, I'd add three more words and make it *the fear of abandonment.* That, too, might make *The Guinness Book of World Records.* But it would miss the mark. For good reason. Most of us are not in touch with our feelings of being abandoned. And so we'd probably ask, *What's that got to do with our battle with fear?* It's got plenty to do with it. Inside all of us there are conscious and buried memories of feelings of abandonment.

Loss in Childhood
Some, like Tim, have lost a parent through divorce. The National Center for Health Statistics presents the grim picture of a divorce rate approach-

ing 50 percent. And what about the children of these broken marriages? No matter how the divorce is explained to them, children usually feel guilty and rejected.

Other adults still feel abandoned from the early loss of one of their parents through death. This loss levels a severe blow to a young person's security, especially if the death occurs during the early teen years.

I remember standing with a fourteen-year-old named Eric, beside the casket of his forty-five-year-old dad, who had died of a massive heart attack. The boy looked me in the eye and sobbed, "How can I ever trust anyone after this? What am I going to do without my dad?"

Eric, now a dynamic Christian businessman, came to see me the other day. It's been twenty years since his dad died. In our conversation he told me about his years of battling fear. He had felt abandoned by his dad and by God. All of the explanations of death and efforts to comfort Eric at the time of his dad's death did not help him. He wanted his dad back!

Only after years of anguished struggle—when he got in touch with his feelings and stopped blaming God—could he be open to hearing about God's love.

Some people can trace their feelings of abandonment back to the prolonged illness of a parent.

That was Melissa's problem. Her mother suffered a long illness after she gave birth to Melissa's younger brother. Melissa was seven at the time and was not allowed to see her mother for several weeks. When she was permitted to enter her mother's sick room in their home, she was told not to touch her. Her mother did not embrace her for months afterward.

All through her adolescent years, Melissa was reminded that her mother was not well. Sometimes when she just needed to talk, she was told that her mother was resting and should not be disturbed. Melissa felt abandoned by her mother even though they lived in the same house.

Sue, a woman in her early thirties, had an even more difficult childhood. Her father's alcoholism taught her not to trust anyone. Her fear of abandonment was rooted in the memories of her father's unpredictable behavior and lack of nurturing love.

Even though Sue had attended a Bible college and seminary, her relationship with God continued to be one of distance and discomfort. There always seemed to be a hollow echo when she called out to God.

"I figured that God was just like my dad," she said. "No matter how hard I tried to reach out to God, His arms always seemed to be a bit short." She went on to say, "I could never really bring myself to look at His face. I was terrified that I would see my own father's angry, scowling face."

In her midtwenties Sue could no longer outrun the emptiness that plagued her. Depression and despair eventually drove her to seek counseling. A loving counselor helped her to see how her father's alcoholism had affected her and how she had transferred her fears of abandonment onto God. She was finally able to allow God to heal her deep wounds.

Some people have suffered something akin to abandonment by suspecting that their parents really cared more for a brother or sister than for them.

Others were damaged when their parents punished them by withdrawing or threatening to withdraw affection. Walter, now sixty years old, felt that type of emotional abandonment. He can still remember his mother threatening that she wouldn't be home when he came home from school unless he got to work and improved his grades. Walter can't shake the memory of running home breathlessly, day after day, wondering if she had kept her threat.

Still other people remember broken familial relationships that have never been healed. Estrangement has much the same emotional impact as abandonment.

Not All in the Family

The sense of abandonment isn't limited to family relationships. We've all had the experience of losing a friend through conflict or unresolved hurts. Being criticized is painful, but being discarded and treated as though we no longer exist is infinitely worse. It disturbs our ability to trust in the future.

The disappointments of life often pile up and give us a discouraged feeling that we've got to face the struggle of life alone. *Who really cares?* many ask in their down times. And then a more disturbing question comes to mind, *Doesn't God know what's happening to me? He must have forgotten me!*

SUPERFICIAL ANSWERS

Superficial Christian teaching has conditioned us to think that the only evidence of God's presence is a constant flow of material blessings and constant "smooth sailing."

Not so. We live in a chaotic world that has fallen from God's perfect plan and is filled with evil people in mutiny against Him. Others couldn't care less about God, and still others are determined to run their own lives. It's also a world in which illness, aging, and death constantly remind us of our mortality.

God has allowed us to be free in this troubled world. We're not puppets; we're people who can use our freedom to choose to love God in response to His love in Christ and His constant care for us.

Trevor has made that choice and expresses it in a vivid way: "In response to the old question, 'How can we trust God in a world like this?' I simply say I couldn't live in a world like this without God. When I think of all the tragic things He's kept from happening and the way He's used the bad things that have happened, I'm amazed. I can't imagine making it without Him."

The truth is that God has called us in the midst of this topsy-turvy world to belong to Him. He understands that our ability to trust Him has been tested by the discouragements and disappointments of life. He knows the painful feelings of abandonment we've endured in the lack of acceptance and affirmation from others.

But He knows something else: He knows how to get through to His beloved people when problems make them wonder if He has turned on them. So here's some really good news!

FEAR NOT

The Lord's constant word to us is "fear not!" There are 366 "fear not!" verses in the Bible—one for every day of the year and an extra one for leap year! Most of the admonitions are followed by a firm assurance of the Lord's presence or a stirring reminder of an aspect of His nature—such as His faithfulness, goodness, loving-kindness, or intervening power in times of need.

Three of these "fear not!" verses are particularly helpful as we begin to practice the principles for living without fear. They were spoken to people who felt abandoned in adversity and needed both the assurance and the experience of the Lord's presence and loving care.

Right in God's Hand

The first two of these "fear not!" verses are actually twin verses from Isaiah 41:10 and 13. The Lord spoke through Isaiah to the captive Israelites in exile. In verse 10 the Lord spoke directly to the people's discouraged sense of abandonment.

> Fear not, for I am with you;
> Be not dismayed, for I am your God.
> I will strengthen you,
> Yes, I will help you,
> I will uphold you with My righteous right hand.

The Hebrew word for *fear* can also be translated "dread." *"Don't dread life because of your circumstances,"* God seemed to say. *"Don't be afraid of your unfamiliar surroundings here in exile away from the securities of Jerusalem and the temple. I am your God; and I am with you in spite of everything!"*

"Be not dismayed" in verse 10 really means "don't look around furtively in panic," as though casting about for some other hope that would bring security or comfort. Looking only to God for help is not an easy task for anyone at any age. How could the people of Israel respond to that statement without the further promise God gave them: "I will uphold you with My righteous right hand"?

In Hebrew, the right hand of God is metaphorical for His presence and power. It is His hand that uplifts us when we are down, upholds us when we are weak, and rouses us when we are sunk in cowardly lethargy.

But note, it's God's *righteous* right hand that takes hold of us in our fears. Here *righteous* means in keeping with God's character, consistent with His nature. In this context God's righteous hand refers to God's grace, God's unlimited care and unqualified love. That's what we need when we feel separated from Him because we fear that He might have forgotten us. When fears so dominate our thinking that we shy away from trusting even God, He invades our self-devised solitary confinement and reveals Himself as our Friend.

How God does that is explained in Isaiah 41:13: "For I, the Lord your God, will hold your right hand, / Saying to you, Fear not, I will help you."

Let's picture that. Suppose that the Lord Jesus extended His right hand to you. I trust you'd respond by offering your right hand. To shake hands properly, the two of you would have to be face to face.

If you stood on His left side, you'd have to reach across Him to get His right hand; conversely, if you stood on His right side, you'd have to reach across your own chest to grasp His right hand.

Who would ever shake the hand of a friend that way? No one. Not if we wanted to communicate with life-or-death intensity.

Instead of an awkward, impersonal, side-by-side grasp of the hand, the Lord takes hold of our right hands with His righteous, grace-filled right hand. That puts us eye to eye with Him. It's exactly what God intends. He has something He wants to say to us that He wants us to hear with the ears of our souls. He wants to get through to that deep inner place in us where fears fester.

"You don't need to be afraid," He says. "I am in charge of your life. I will never leave or forsake you. Trust Me. Take this first step to living without fear. I am Jehovah-Shammah, the Lord Is There. And wherever you are, be more sure of this than you are of your next breath: I will be there."

Right in God's Presence

The third "fear not!" verse that I want to address was spoken by Jesus to the disciples when they were caught in a raging, turbulent storm on the Sea of Galilee (see Jn 6:15-21). They were terrified.

Storms on the Sea of Galilee are often violent. The strong winds howl through the gorges in the mountains, which act like wind tunnels, concentrating the blasts of gale on the sea.

The disciples had ridden out many a storm on the sea. But this was unlike any storm they had faced before. It lasted nine hours. And during those dangerous hours, the disciples rowed only three or four of the six miles across the sea.

If only Jesus were with us now! they must have thought. A few hours before, they had witnessed His miracle of the feeding of the five thousand. He had retreated to the mountain, and the disciples had set off across the sea for Capernaum. "If the Master could multiply a few loaves and fishes to feed a huge crowd, He could save us now!"

Then Jesus miraculously approached them, walking on the water. That He could come to them as if the angry sea were dry ground was enough reason for awe. But the words He spoke filled them with both wonder and worship. Above the howling of the wind and the surging of the sea, Jesus spoke with divine authority that rolled like thunder. "It is I; do not be afraid" (Jn 6:20).

Jesus then got into the disciples' boat, and they immediately made it to the shore. The men never forgot those words. Nor can we.

The English translation of Jesus' fear-liberating words doesn't do justice to the true meaning. In the Greek it is *Ego eimi me phobeisthe.* I am convinced that this is one of Jesus' twenty-two "I am" assertions. I like to translate it, "I am; have no fear." In the Greek version of the Exodus passages of the Old Testament, *Ego eimi,* I Am, was used to translate God's name, *Yahweh*. When Jesus said, "Before Abraham was, I Am" (Jn 8:58), the Gospel uses the same *Ego eimi*.

For me, the literal impact of the words spoken to the disciples is, "It is I, Yahweh, have no fear." Jesus claimed to be none other than God with them, Emmanuel.

THE LORD IS HERE

Christ comes to you and me in our lonely fear with all power and authority. He will not leave us helpless in the restless sea of life.

Sometimes this means that the Lord rides out the storm with us. Other times, to our delight, He calms the restless sea around us. But first and foremost, He calms the storm inside us—in our deepest inner soul. And when He does, we can begin to face all of the fears that disturb our thinking, in our personal relationships and responsibilities, and in our culture.

I experienced that peace when I first invited Christ to live in me as a freshman in college. The following summer I went fishing in Canada with my dad, who had recently renewed his faith in Christ. The Lord used our time together to bind us into a deeper relationship than we'd ever known.

While we were fishing, a storm came up and thrashed the lake with dangerous waves. We were tossed about like a cork on the lake. Our small motor boat nearly capsized.

Then, when we had nearly given up hope of surviving, suddenly the wind subsided; in a few minutes the lake was flat as a mirror.

Dad and I looked at each other. Then he said quietly, "Lloyd, the Lord is here!" And indeed He was.

But I'm no less convinced that the Lord has been with me when the storms around me didn't cease. The sea He calms at such times is inside my soul. With His peace replacing our fears, we can take anything.

So fear not! You belong to the Lord, and He has promised, "I will never leave you nor forsake you" (Heb 13:5). Now claim that promise and know that the Lord will never abandon you.

Chapter Two

WHOM SHALL I FEAR?

One Thursday in my weekly Bible study with senators, our study of Scripture led us to the passage, "The fear of the Lord is the beginning of wisdom" (Ps 111:10). Careful review of the Hebrew reminded us that the word translated *beginning* means "better part." So the verse might read: "The fear of the Lord is the *better part* of wisdom."

One of the senators said, "Chaplain, you've been helping us learn to love God more. Now you tell us we need to fear Him in order to receive the gift of wisdom. Isn't that a contradiction?"

I tried to explain that *fear* in this context means awe and wonder. I could see the lights go on in their minds. Awe and wonder before God is the prelude to receiving the gift of wisdom. It is a discovery we all need to make, again and again.

There's a disturbing loss of awe and wonder in our contemporary understanding of our relationship with God. We've dropped the bracing biblical phrase "the fear of the Lord" from our list of Christian virtues.

That's frightening. Literally. Terror grips us when we lose our fear of God. Without that one creative fear, we have no defense against all our destructive fears.

I'm not talking about a cringing anguish before a tyrannical God but about awe and wonder that is expressed in adoration, praise, and obedience. The Holy God is our Creator and Judge as well as our Redeemer and Friend.

FALSE GODS

Our reverence is misspent when it is squandered on anything or anyone other than the Lord God. Debilitating fear pervades our thoughts and feelings when we sneak around the first commandment: "You shall have no other gods before Me" (Ex 20:3). Idolatry means giving to any person, purpose, or plan the ultimate allegiance and control that really belong to God.

Unfortunately, we tend to elevate the things and people we fear to the status of false gods. When we fear certain people and need their approval too much, we seek to please and placate them as if they were the source of our worth. They become little gods in our lives.

The same can be true of our families, careers, money, reputation, health, and the accomplishments of our past or our dreams for the future. Anything or anyone we cannot bear the thought of losing becomes enthroned with godlike status in our lives.

That's a painful, disturbing thought. As uncomfortable as it may be, test it out. Reflect on what makes you afraid. Could it be that this very thing or person is competing with the Lord God for first place in your life? When we think about that, we want to pray with the eighteenth-century poet William Cowper:

The dearest idol I have known,
Whate'er that idol be;
Help me to tear it from Thy throne,
And worship only Thee.

The first prescription for living without fear was to trust that God will never leave nor forsake you. His presence with us not only gives us comfort and courage but also leads us to a great challenge. God wants to claim our misdirected reverence and set us free to love and serve Him above all else.

That leads us to our next prescription: *Overcome your crippling fears with a creative fear of God expressed in awe and wonder, adoration and faithful obedience. He is the only Person you have to please.*

Dread Versus Reverence

In the Bible there's a distinction between dread and reverence, but it's easy to get confused because one Hebrew word has both meanings. The most common Hebrew verb for fear, *yārē*, signifies having godly reverence, living in obedience, or experiencing human terror.

For example, in Genesis 15:1 God appeared to Abram and said, "Do not be afraid [of Me]." In Deuteronomy 6:2 Moses told the people that the commandments and provisions of God had been given "that you may fear the Lord your God." And the psalmist said, "Blessed is the man who fears the Lord" (Ps 112:1). All three passages use the same verb, *yārē*.

There's a similar pattern in the Greek New Testament; *phobos* refers both to terror and dread and also to reverential fear. Jesus' command to the disciples to "fear not!" which we considered in the previous chapter, used a word closely related to *phobos*. *Phobos* was used also to describe the quality of reverence of the early church: "And walking in the fear of the Lord and in the comfort of the Holy Spirit, they were multiplied" (Acts 9:31). The

Greek word *deilia* refers specifically to cowardly fear (see 2 Tm 1:7) and *eulabeia* to holy fear (see Heb 5:7; 12:28), but generally throughout the New Testament *phobos* is employed to express both good and bad fear.

So in both the Old and New Testaments, we must look at the context to discover which sort of fear we are reading about. The thrust of each passage will make clear whether it refers to constructive or debilitating fear.

Reverential awe plays a crucial part in bringing us into a right relationship with our Holy God. It is in this relationship of complete trust and submission that we receive the power to overcome our fears. Without that relationship we will have to wage a lonely battle with fear, relying on our own resources.

Solomon said, "The fear of the Lord is the beginning of knowledge" (Prv 1:7). Here again is that Hebrew word that might be translated "choice part" or "chief part." And so we can paraphrase Solomon's words, "Awe, wonder, and humility are the choice, chief part of knowing God." Everything else flows from that healthy fear.

DIFFERENT REACTIONS TO THE FEAR OF GOD

There are four possible reactions to the fear of God. The first three make us children of a false god who is really no god at all. The fourth shows us how to become fearless children of the true God. Let me explain and illustrate what I mean with the stories of four very different people. Many of us will identify with one of the first three. My prayer is that we'll all discover the liberating and creative fear experienced by the fourth.

Paralyzed by the Dread of God
Some Christians have had an overdose of wrong understanding of the fear of God. They cannot glorify or enjoy God, because they have been taught to dread Him rather than adore and love Him with humble trust.

Adam was raised in a legalistically religious family. He was taught to be afraid of God. In practical terms that meant he was conditioned to dread the wrath of an angry, judgmental God. And yet he had to try to please God by following, to the letter, the rigid rules of his parents' brand of Christianity.

As a result of this childhood conditioning, Adam developed a very cautious attitude toward life. Adam cannot ever remember feeling God's love and forgiveness, and he finds it difficult to imagine ever being close to God.

The upshot of all this is that Adam does not feel awe and wonder over the majesty and goodness of God, but rather a shrinking aversion that has only multiplied his fears that he will do something that displeases God.

Rebelling Against an Angry God

Fear of an angry God can cause a second type of reaction: rebellion, a "who needs this?" reaction. Martha had a background much like Adam's, but her response was quite different. She remembers that her parents kept her in line by threatening her with judgment and punishment from God. When she went away to college and got out of the grip of their control, she declared her independence from them and from the "cosmic policeman" god she had been taught to fear.

Because Martha never replaced the negative conditioning she received with a positive faith, she is filled with a floating sense of fear. She has an overactive conscience, but she has nowhere to turn in times of failure or in the midst of demanding pressures.

Recently Martha said, "Lloyd, I'm afraid that life is like a courtroom without a judge. There's no objectivity, no standard, no edge on which to cut. It's all dependent on me. I am left to decide what is right, and I'm not always sure. I feel lonesome and afraid.

"I don't want to go back to my parents' religion and all that fear. I thought I was getting away from fear. But now I have more than ever."

Being Ignorant of the Fear of the Lord

By far the largest number of Christians today would fit into a third group. Unlike Adam and Martha, they've never had to wrestle with a misinterpretation of what it really means to fear the Lord. They've never heard much about it. The churches they attend seldom, if ever, mention it.

The emphasis of much contemporary Christianity is on God's acceptance, with far too little teaching about our accountability to Him. Phil was raised in that type of shallow Christianity. He believed in God and said his prayers, but his spiritual growth was stunted.

I met Phil at an executive leadership seminar at which I spoke. In our conversations I soon discovered why his faith was shallow. The god of his life was his career; reverence and awe had been replaced by his passion for success. Phil achieved great success early in life and accumulated many status symbols. Yet his life was unsatisfying and joyless.

Los Angeles Times writer Betty Cuniberti aptly described the problem of people like Phil. "They are well stocked with MBAs, VCRs, and BMWs. But they are SAD," Cuniberti wrote. "Many ... find their jobs long on salary, short on satisfaction.... Their Victorian homes may be stuffed with high-tech gadgetry but the owners feel empty inside."[1]

Phil's emptiness was real. It showed up in lots of fears. He was worried about failure and about not being able to keep up with his friends.

Raised in a traditional Christian home, Phil was taught that God loved and cared for him. But he missed two important truths. First, he failed to understand that God had a plan for his life. Second, he failed to realize that he was responsible to God for the use of his extensive talents and intelligence.

For Phil, God was a sort of benevolent, permissive "Uncle Joe." He prayed to God in times of need and expected help to accomplish his own plans and purposes. Phil's values and lifestyle were conditioned by culture and not by his faith. And yet, at thirty-five, Phil was wondering, *Is this all there is?*

Oscar Wilde said that there are two sources of unhappiness in life. "One is not getting what one wants, and the other is getting it." Phil got what he thought he wanted, but in the process he almost closed himself off from the Father's judgment and healing.

Having a Healthy Fear of God

The fourth group has a healthy experience of the fear of God. They don't swagger in God's presence; they fall on their knees. They believe in a holy God in whose presence they worship with wonder and praise regarding His power and greatness. They know that they could not come into His glorious presence except by His invitation. He is infinite, eternal, and unchangeable. He alone is God in His majesty, wisdom, goodness, justice, and truth. Only He can make the absolute demand for our obedience and provide the supernatural power to accomplish it according to His will.

God is also our Judge.

In a culture dominated by children of lesser gods, that truth may not win a popularity contest, but it must be said. We are accountable to our Father for what we do with what He has entrusted to us—our own lives, the lives of people around us, and the magnificent natural world in which He has etched His signature with grandeur.

THE POSITIVE RESULTS OF HEALTHY FEAR OF THE LORD

Healthy fear of the Lord generates very positive results. That's the promise the psalmist gives in one of my favorite verses about the fear of the Lord: "The secret of the Lord is with those who fear Him, / And He will show them His covenant" (Ps 25:14).

The Hebrew word translated as *secret* really means "friendship." Spurgeon said it implies "confidential intimacy and select fellowship."

What does God do when we come to Him with reverent fear? He welcomes us as friends and shows us His covenant. A covenant is a promise that establishes a relationship of mutual trust. The psalmist is speaking, of course, of the covenant the Lord made with Abraham and later confirmed to the nation of Israel, "I will ... be your God and you shall be My people" (Lv 26:12).

But we become the Lord's people under a new and better covenant. God comes to us in Christ, Emmanuel, "God With Us." He comes first in judgment and then in grace. He confronts us with what we are and then with what He has destined us to be. Again we respond with awe and wonder. He knows all about us!

The depth of God's love is revealed in this covenant. He reconciles us to Himself through Christ's death. When we experience the Father's wondrous love for us, we are filled with even greater awe than before. As Paul joyfully expressed it, "You did not receive the spirit of bondage again to fear [dread], but you received the Spirit of adoption by whom we cry out, 'Abba, Father'" (Rom 8:15). No longer do we dread God but call Him by the most intimate of names. We rejoice with sheer astonishment over His glory and His reconciling love.

THE NEW PHIL

Earlier I promised that I would illustrate this fourth group with the story of a person who has experienced this healthy fear of the Lord. You may be surprised that it's the "rest of the story" of Phil.

A few paragraphs ago we left him trapped in his fears of failure, urgently needing a genuine experience of the fear of the Lord. I'm thankful Phil's story didn't end there.

The essence of healthy fear of the Lord is humility. Phil's real problem was that his lesser god was himself. No wonder he became fearful! With all his gifts he could accomplish almost anything with superb excellence. Except one thing: He couldn't be Lord over his own life.

When Phil realized how far he'd fallen short of God's plan for him, he became filled with holy fear. He saw how preoccupied he'd been with his self-serving lust for success. With anguish he reviewed the way he'd used people as rungs in his arrogant climb up the ladder of success. Especially disturbing for him was the way he had hurt his lovely wife, whom he had treated like one of the many things he had accumulated to fortify his image of accomplishment.

Added to this, Phil was deeply moved by the witness of some dynamic Christian executives. The Lord had led them and their companies to become involved in community problems, human suffering, and world hunger. Phil had to admit that he'd been living in his own little world while soul-sized issues swirled around him. Influenced by these executives, he saw how irrelevant his life really was when compared to what God was up to in the world. Phil's pride was being broken by a holy fear; he was ready to hear with new ears the gospel of God's love in Christ.

All this led to a dramatic recommitment to Christ. And the transformation is not over. I suggested that Phil spend fifteen minutes every morning reading the Bible and reflecting on the greatness and glory of God, and then report in for duty to serve Him.

In a recent conversation on the phone, Phil exclaimed, "Lloyd, what a puny God I had! It was like shutting myself up in a three-foot by seven-foot hut on the floor of the Grand Canyon. As God kicked in the door, blew off the roof, and knocked down the walls, I beheld His grandeur and glory." I've heard conversions described in lots of ways, but never as vividly as that.

Phil, a child of a lesser god, has become a man of the holy Lord God. And the same Lord God wants nothing less for you and me.

Many years ago writer and pastor James Fordyce shared the secret of how awe and wonder cure our sapping fears:

> Henceforth the majesty of God revere,
> Fear Him and you have nothing else to fear.

Chapter Three

WHO'S HOME?

PRESCRIPTION 3:

Face your fears; retrace them to their source in your heart; displace them by making your heart Christ's home; and erase them with God's perfect love.

When I arrived at my Senate office one morning, the first reminder on my typed agenda stood out in bold letters: *Call your granddaughter, Erin!* She had called and wanted to talk personally with me. We finally connected at 4:30 P.M. California time; 7:30 P.M. Washington time. "Erin, is everything all right?" I asked with concern.

"Sure, Grandpa. You keep your promises, don't you? Well, remember that evening when you took me to the Lincoln Memorial? We stood there together reading the Gettysburg Address on the wall, and you promised that if I memorized it, you would give me one hundred dollars. So, are you ready? 'Fourscore and seven years ago ...'"

My heart swelled with pride, and my eyes filled with tears as thirteen-year-old Erin repeated the entire address perfectly. When she finished, I told her how impressed I was and how much I loved her. The one hundred dollars would be on its way in the morning.

The next day, I went to the bank and got a crisp new hundred-dollar bill and overnighted it to Erin. When she called again, she said, "Grandpa, do you know what it's like to have a hundred dollars?! Thank you! I am putting seventy-five dollars into savings and using the other twenty-five dollars to give a party for the other kids in my class who also memorized the Gettysburg Address."

The ensuing conversation was filled with tender moments of affirmation and delight.

When I see my four grandchildren, Erin, Airley, Bonnie, and Scotter, they run to greet me. How I cherish them and appreciate them! When I hug them, I realize how much I love them. Then I think of God's love for them. If I multiplied my love billions of times, I would touch only the edge of the immensity of His love for my precious grandchildren.

Then it hits me. If my grandchildren can bring that much pleasure to me, is it possible that I bring pleasure to my heavenly Father's heart? Again I ponder the infinite, incalculable depth of God's love and ask myself, *Can I run to God with the same childlike freedom and enthusiasm that my grandchildren express when they run to me? Can I let go and allow God to hold me with loving acceptance and assurance?*

Often we can't. Just thinking about the things we've said or done makes us feel unworthy. This causes us to feel that God should meet us with the stiff arm of judgment rather than the open arms of acceptance.

We project our own self-condemnation onto God. When we need Him the most, we feel estranged. There is an uneasy distance between Him and us.

But when we feel this separation from God, who moved? Did God? No! We did! His love toward us has not changed, but our attitude toward Him has become strained and cautious. We feel an aching emptiness.

It's then that our hearts become a landlord to an unruly tenant. Fear takes up residence and begins to act as if it owns the house of our inner soul.

This fear is very different from the awe and wonder discussed in the previous chapter. Rather, it is a cold dread, a feeling of discord and jangled unrest.

I am convinced that this deep, inner fear is the root of our lesser, external fears. It gets focused on frightening situations, alarming circumstances, and troublesome people. All efforts to overcome our surface fears will be ineffective until this deepest fear is exposed and healed.

GETTING TO THE ROOT OF THE PROBLEM

At root, what we think we fear is usually not what we fear. One of the basic causes of fear is self-inflicted estrangement from God. We were created to know Him, experience His unqualified love, love Him in return, and enjoy an intimate fellowship with Him. If we never come to know Him or if our relationship with Him has been only a vague religious belief in Him or if we have drifted away from Him in willful independence, the gaping cavern in our souls will be filled with this most profound of all fears—fear of judgment and estrangement from God.

At its core, this basic fear is really a manifestation of guilt. It is the universal and inevitable human reaction to being separated from God.

You may be surprised that I've used the word *guilt* to describe that condition. Over the years, in deep conversations with people about their inner thoughts and feelings, I have discovered that many have a sense of incompleteness, as if they were created for something they haven't yet discovered or achieved. Unable to grasp a greater purpose in life, they feel out of sync. Something—they're not sure what—is wrong.

This floating sense that things are not quite right is the tug of God in our souls. No amount of human reassurance and affirmation will heal the unrest. Achievement and success cannot relieve the insecurity and anxiety. God is creating in us a longing for Himself, and the disjointed, fragmented sense of alienation will persist until we know His unconditional love and acceptance and discover His will for our lives.

This general floating sense of guilt is soon attached to our mistakes and failures. We end up feeling down on ourselves because of what we've done or said. That motivates the fear of judgment and punishment. The strange twist is that this guilt prompts many people to run from, rather than into, the accepting and reconciling arms of God. By refusing to submit to God's judgment, we close ourselves off from His reconciling love, the only source of healing for fear.

A vicious circle results. Guilt causes us to fear punishment; we either condemn ourselves or begin self-justifying improvement programs; our guilt deepens as we become further alienated from God, starting the circle all over again.

THE TORMENTING CONNECTION

The apostle John reveals the secret of overcoming fear in his first epistle to the Christians in the Roman province of Asia Minor. Though they believed in God, many of them were waging a losing battle with fear.

They faced rejection because of their faith, the constant threat of persecution, and the demeaning influence of false teachers who tried to undermine their trust in Christ's atoning death and empowering presence. This was coupled with opposition from a godless, secular culture, and conflict with pagan religions. Added to these fear-inducing situations were the pressures and difficulties of daily living.

Like us, they tended to blame people and problems for their fears.

In one of the most concise and penetrating statements in Scripture, John showed first-century Christians how their external fears were attached to a deeper fear. What he wrote can give contemporary Christians an understanding of the origin of fear. "There is no fear in love," John tells us, "but perfect love casts out fear, because fear involves torment. But he who fears has not been made perfect in love" (1 Jn 4:18).

Let's consider John's basic insight about negative fear. The Greek word translated as *fear* here and throughout this verse is *phobos,* meaning panic, dread, and terror. This root fear, according to John, is caused by torment.

The Greek word is *ross*. It means punishment or discipline. The torment is our fear of impending judgment.

I believe that this fear is inherent in all human beings. It is called by many names—anxiety, nervousness, incompleteness, a sense of inadequacy, a floating sense of guilt. At base it is a fractured relationship with the God who made us for Himself. He pursues us, and the closer He presses on our soul, the more we feel our emptiness. Believe it or not, that emptiness is a gift of grace.

THE GNAWING UNEASINESS

Strange as it may seem, the inner sense of separation from God is felt by many of those who believe in Him. I meet them everywhere. They are faithful church members, successful professionals, even pastors and Christian leaders. And yet they are unsure of God's unlimited grace for them.

Allen is a good example. His story shows the plight of good people who are suddenly confronted with fear and discover that in spite of being religious they are alienated from God.

Allen was raised by good, moral parents. From early childhood they taught him to believe in God and to try to please Him. The way to do that, they told him, was to do what was "right." That "right" was interpreted to him in the rules and regulations his parents set down. They praised him when he measured up and punished him when he failed.

God was established as the higher authority in his family life. Prayers of gratitude for God's daily blessings were said at every meal. What Allen's parents did not have, and therefore could not expose him to, was an intimate relationship with God. They were self-reliant, responsible people who taught him to work hard and to use the talents God had given him.

Allen's parents were leaders in their local church. Allen was enrolled in the church school at an early age and was awarded the gold star for perfect attendance right through his teen years. He was confirmed at fourteen and became a leader in the scout troop and youth fellowship.

The amazing thing is that, with all this religious training, Allen cannot remember ever being taught about how to know God personally. God's love was presented in His goodness and providential care. Allen believed that God would help him live out the clear moral integrity his parents had taught him. At no time was he confronted with the fact that, in spite of his model behavior, he was separated from God in the depth of his being.

After college Allen's talents, excellent mind, and industriousness made him a sought-after employee. Soon he achieved executive responsibility and was on his way to financial and social success. He married Eileen, an outstanding woman who shared his values and goals. Together they pursued successful careers.

You may have leaped ahead of the story and pictured some personal or professional crisis that brought Allen to a realization of his need for a profound experience of God's grace. Wrong. There were no tragedies, moral failures, or marital problems.

God is wonderfully original in the way He works with each of us. For some, life must fall apart before we realize how much we need Him. It happened differently for Allen. At age forty he became aware of a gnawing uneasiness. At first he wrote it off as a midlife crisis. He changed jobs, moved to another city, and got busy in community activities. Still he felt turmoil in the pit of his stomach.

One Friday evening, as Allen sat alone at his desk, a terrible fear gripped him that he could not shake. It triggered a feeling of dread. Though he had tried to do all of the right things, he felt wrong. An inescapable sense of guilt flooded him. *Why do I feel this way?* he wondered. *I believe in God and have tried to live a good life. What's wrong?* Later that evening Allen shared this experience with his wife. She had felt some of the same anxiety but had never told him. One word described her feelings: *emptiness.*

Amazing. Here were two successful people who were both feeling fear they had never confided to each other. Now that they had been honest with each other, what could they do about their mutual need? Take a trip? Redecorate their house? Find a new hobby?

I'm thankful that before they ran off in all directions seeking to fill their emptiness with new activities or possessions, God intervened.

THE TURNING POINT

One Sunday morning while having breakfast, Allen and Eileen watched one of my messages on television. That program, though taped weeks before, was perfectly timed by God for them.

I spoke about the plight of the good person who misses the full measure of God's love because of self-righteousness. Then I went on to talk about the joy of an intimate relationship with God through Christ. That was contrasted with the emptiness of good people who do all the right things but still are sinners who need to be reconciled with God. I felt compelled to explain that often the working of the Spirit of God produces a disquieting dissatisfaction with life, then anxiety, and finally a sense of fear.

At the end of the message I gave some clear steps on how to admit one's emptiness and accept God's unlimited love in Christ. I described how listeners could surrender their fears to Christ, ask Him to fill them with His Spirit, and commit their lives to Him.

When the program was over, Allen said to Eileen, "How did that preacher know about us? The message was just for us!" Soon after I met with them, and we had the first of several good visits together. Finally, both Allen and Eileen made a commitment to Christ and asked to be filled with His Spirit.

There are millions of people like this couple. They profess to be Christians and try to live a good life, but they remain estranged from the Lord in their deep inner hearts. They have little assurance of His love and acceptance. Their hearts are filled with insecurity and self-judgment. The resulting fear becomes focused on situations, people, and frightening possibilities. They are the ones who know all of the words but none of the music.

The great Southern novelist Walker Percy observed that "a person can get all A's and still flunk life." Like Allen and Eileen, who did all the right things but still felt the emptiness of fear and separation, all of us need to be brought to our knees in prayer. When we surrender our fears to Christ—when we forget about being perfect before God on our own strength and when we ask Him to fill us with the life-giving power of His Spirit—our lives will be better than a mere passing grade. We will know that the loving purpose of our lives is to enjoy an intimate, personal relationship with God, the Lord of Life!

MORE THAN HALF-HEALED

God does not want to leave us half-healed, with a vague concept of His loving-kindness that does not penetrate to our inner guilt. He knows the plight of the "good" person who talks about God's love and still lives in what Henry David Thoreau called the "quiet desperation" of guilt-induced, hidden fear. God wants to break through the barrier of the protective, partial truth that He loves us just "as we are." His love for us "as we are" also includes healing the guilt that has made us the fearful people we are.

Let's get back to John's potent five-word prescription for receiving God's love for the healing of this fear in our innermost souls: *"Perfect love casts out fear."*

We've heard and seen these five words before. We see them printed on posters and artfully arranged with colorful calligraphy on greeting cards. We get a warm feeling of assurance when we hear or see them. They seem to hold out a wonderful promise if we could only grasp it.

But merely saying these words doesn't remove our fears. Some people find that the promise actually adds to their insecurity. Perfect love? Who can achieve that? And others wonder what the promise really means.

Does the knowledge that we are loved really eradicate our fears? If so, why are so many people who have heard about God's love still filled with fear? And what's more, why do those who have experienced His gracious provision and care continue to wrestle with distressing fears?

I think it is because most of us have misunderstood the true meaning of the word *perfect*.

PERFECT LOVE

The Greek word for perfect, *teleios*, describes that which has reached its end, has accomplished its purpose, and is completed, fully grown, and mature. With this definition in mind, we can understand that God's love for us accomplishes its purpose whenever it heals our guilt, gives us the certainty of our security in Christ, or fills us with a complete confidence that we have been accepted in spite of what we've said or done.

We experience God's perfect love in what He did and does through Christ; He came to humankind when we could no longer come to Him because of the alienation caused by guilt.

Christ was and is God's Love accomplishing its goal: the reconciliation of His fearful children to Himself. The Master taught, modeled, and revealed the loving heart of the Father. And then, as the Savior of the world, He chose to suffer and die not just for our *sins* but for our sin: the guilt-motivated refusal to be loved and to love the Father in return.

On the cross Christ endured not only the excruciating physical pain of the crucifixion but also the incalculable anguish of being separated from God. He took our guilt onto Himself. And there, during those hours on the cross, He received the full impact of the judgment of God. As the Lamb of God was nailed to that cruel cross, He was thinking of you and me, as well as of His executioners. "Father, forgive them, for they do not know what they do" (Lk 23:34). The Roman soldiers didn't realize they were participants in the event that would free humankind from the penalty of sin. Nor do we when we harbor guilt and fear as if Jesus had never died.

At high noon on that tragic Friday, darkness enshrouded Golgotha. For the three longest hours in history, Jesus suffered estrangement from the Father. As Paul put it, "He made Him who knew no sin to be sin for us, that we might become the righteousness of God in Him" (2 Cor 5:21). That was God's purpose—to make us right with Him. When those hours of darkness were finished, Christ sobbed out the reality of what He had been through. "My God, My God, why have You forsaken Me?" (Mk 15:34). The sacrifice of His life brought forth a new creation.

No wonder He shouted in triumph, "It is finished!" (Jn 19:30). Indeed it was. It was complete, never to be repeated. Perfect, for then, for now, and forever. And it's for you and me.

VERDICT: NOT GUILTY

With the authority of God and the credentials of His cross, Jesus Christ pronounces us not guilty. He takes away our guilt for what we've been as well as what we've done. Graciously, He gives us the gift of faith to accept His forgiveness and be set free from our fear. John was right. Fear has to do with torment. But Christ, perfect Love Himself, casts it out.

Love and fear cannot coexist together. As John explained, the person who fears has not been made perfect in love. Unresolved guilt is still the breeding ground for fear within us. The good news is that Christ never lets up on us until we are liberated.

When we invite Christ to live in us, He, as perfect Love, displaces our fear. Daily, moment by moment, within our hearts, He washes away our feelings of guilt and dislodges our fear. He stands guard at the entrance to our hearts with a no-vacancy sign in His hand. It is His plan and goal constantly to evict that unruly tenant, fear, from our hearts and replace it with His own presence.

EVICTING THE TENANT

Most of us would probably have to admit that fear still "sleeps" in our hearts some nights. We know love can't be a roommate with fear, and yet...

When we know that the Lord will never leave or forsake us and that He will not take second place to our lesser gods, we are ready to confront our need for Him to remove our guilt-oriented fear.

The third prescription for fearless living is designed to help you do just that: Face your fears; retrace them to their source in your heart; displace them by making your heart Christ's home; and erase them with God's perfect love.

Face It

Face your fears, don't submerge them.

There are two undeniable things about our fears. They are real to us, and they won't go away simply by wishing them away. So we ask, *What is it in my life that causes me to fear? What makes me feel insecurity, alarm, or uncertainty?*

I find that my external fears all fall into one or more of the following categories. Each one begins with the letter P: people, problems, perplexities, possibilities. How does that square with your experience? Whatever it is, step up to it and look it squarely in the eye.

Retrace It

Next, retrace your fears. Refocus in your mind's eye the source of your present fears. What deeper anxiety lurks behind the present situation, circumstance, or relationship that is making you fearful? Is it some person who injured you or some past failure that is causing you to fear the future? Remember, if we don't deal with the past, we will compulsively repeat it.

In retracing our fears it is important for us to remember that what we think we fear is usually not what we fear at all. Most of our external fears are rooted in our deeper guilt-motivated fear that is the result of alienation from God. We have gnawing feelings of guilt not just because of things we've done, but because we willfully avoid intimacy with the Lord.

Displace It

After facing and retracing our fears, the next step is to ask Christ to move in and live in our hearts. This opens the way for Him to have authority in our hearts.

We can't evict fear on our own. Only Christ can do that. The secret is to focus on Him and not on our fears. In doing that we will deliberately refuse to spend time rehashing our fears.

My friend Terry Teykl expressed it using a photographer's simile: "Fear is the darkroom in which we develop our negatives of frightening possibilities." But when we allow the Lord to flood our dark rooms with the brilliant light of His presence, our fears are dispelled completely. We can picture ourselves as the person Christ wants us to be.

Erase It

Finally, only Christ can erase our fears. It's His miracle. Our part is to pray, "Lord, I don't want this fear anymore. I don't want to hang onto it as a false security any longer. I ask You to erase it and clean it off the blackboard of my memory."

How the Lord answers that prayer is the exciting thing I want to share in the next chapter about the healing of memories.

Chapter Four

LEFT LUGGAGE?

> ## PRESCRIPTION 4:
> *Let go of hurting memories from the past. Do not anticipate the repetition of past pain; accept forgiveness from the Lord; and forgive everything and everyone from the past—including yourself.*

G reat Britain's railway stations, airports, and hotels have traditionally provided places called Left Luggage. They are exactly what the words imply—a designated area to leave luggage for a time.

I was reminded of this unique *left luggage* term while spending study leave in Scotland. After a time of concentrated study in my hideaway hotel, I decided to interrupt my work for a few days of fishing. All I would need for that brief interlude was some warm clothing and my fishing equipment. But since I would be giving up my room while I was away, the rest of my clothing, as well as my books and papers, had to be packed in a trunk.

When I was ready to leave, I called Frank, the hall porter, and asked him to check the trunk into the hotel's "Left Luggage." When Frank arrived at my door to get the trunk, he wanted to know where I was going, how long I would be gone, and whether I intended to come back for my trunk. Then he said, "We've had guests who've abandoned their 'left luggage' here for months. Some of them never pick it up."

I assured Frank that I'd be away for only a few days and that I really needed to forget about the unfinished work in the trunk for a while. He completely missed my point. His parting reminder was, "Mind you, don't forget your left luggage!"

Frank's reminder not to forget my left luggage came back to my mind all too often while I was trying to catch an elusive salmon in the Dee River. In fact, worry over the work I had left behind kept me from enjoying the fishing. Finally, I said to myself, *The Lord has given you these few days to rest and relax. Now forget the left luggage!*

Reflecting on that experience makes me think about the place in our memories that might be called "left luggage." It's filled with the troublesome memories we wish we could forget. Instead of resolving them, we simply store them away. They are still there to haunt us. They cripple us from freely moving on into the future.

Years ago, when passengers routinely crossed the Atlantic by ship, a passenger's cases and trunks containing items not needed during the time on board were tagged, "Not needed for the voyage." Just so, many of our memories are unnecessary for our voyage into a future of freedom. We especially do not need the memories that remind us of our failures or of things others have said and done to hurt us.

FORGETTING TO REMEMBER AND REMEMBERING TO FORGET

All too often we remember what we'd like to forget and forget what we need to remember.

In my work as chaplain of the Senate, I keep a list of the people for whom I've promised to pray. A sacred trust is established when I say to a person, "I'll be praying for you." But a real test of the authenticity of that promise is to be able to say, "I've prayed daily about that need you shared with me." With all the needs from senators and staff confided to me each day, I'd be in real trouble trying to remember them all in my morning devotions if I did not keep a list—sometimes even lists to remind me of lists!

I remember a time I forgot something very important. When I was a pastor in Bethlehem, Pennsylvania, I had a small study in the basement of our home. One night I was burning the midnight oil. My concentration was interrupted by a gentle knock at the door of the study. There, attired in purple loveliness (which I will not describe in full detail!), stood my wife, Mary Jane. She held a little present in her hand, beautifully wrapped in purple paper (her favorite color) with a purple bow and purple note. With a beaming smile on her face, she handed it to me. I opened the note and read the words written in—you guessed it—purple ink: "Happy Anniversary. I love you." I had completely forgotten!

I've been known to forget other important things. One Saturday afternoon a call from the wedding hostess reminded me of a wedding half an hour away and saved my reputation.

I pride myself on preaching without notes. I'm thankful for a good memory. Even so, I've forgotten carefully memorized paragraphs of manuscripts and have finished repeating a poem with words and meter the poet would not have recognized! After something like that happens, I usually work all the harder to develop an accurate memory.

But I have to admit there are also times when I wish my memory were not so accurate. Like everyone, I keep some items in my "left luggage" that I need to forget. All of us have some memories we hope will never be exposed. Unfortunately, these skeletons rattle in the closets of our minds and remind us that we have not forgotten. In addition to the memories of our own failures are the memories of how others have failed us.

One of the greatest causes of fear in our lives is holding on to the past. The panic over being discovered for what we've done, combined with memories of hurts from others, produces a feeling of uneasiness about the past and fear of the future.

This brings us to the next liberating prescription for living without fear; it's easier to state this prescription than to take it. We can't do it alone. But the Lord will help us.

Let go of hurting memories from the past. Do not anticipate the repetition of past pain; accept forgiveness from the Lord; and forgive everything and everyone from the past—including yourself.

Remember, the Lord wants us to conquer the fear of the past, so we can be free to live in the present and reach out to others who are still in bondage. He takes us by the hand as we take the next step.

GOD FORGIVES AND FORGETS

We will be able to take this momentous step if we consider another glorious aspect of God's nature: His memory and His ability to forget. One of His great attributes is that He deliberately forgets our failures but never forgets about us. That's so astounding that I hasten to assure you it's not my idea but God's own revelation about Himself in the Bible.

In Isaiah 43:18-19 the Lord tells us what to forget and why:

Do not remember the former things,
Nor consider the things of old.
Behold, I will do a new thing.
Now it shall spring forth;
Shall you not know it?

And why should we forget the old things? The Lord says,

I, even I, am He who blots out your transgressions for My own sake;
And I will not remember your sins.
Put Me in remembrance;
Let us contend together;
State your case, that you may be acquitted.

ISAIAH 43:25-26

We can forget the past by remembering the Lord. We must remember that He has forgotten our sins and failures. And yet we must confess them specifically if we are to be healed. At His command we must march through the prison of our memories, extracting each captive memory and presenting it for display before Him. When we state our own case against ourselves, we can then be acquitted. All of our mistakes and all the injustices that have wounded us will be brought into the court of His presence. Then as we finish our condemnatory judgment of ourselves and others, He will say, "I forgot that long ago; now you are free to forget it."

No one can take grace lightly. God's promise to forget has been sealed with Jesus' blood, shed on the cross. Throughout the Old Testament, His repeated assurances, "I will remember your sins no more," express His forgiving-forgetting heart and also look forward to Calvary. When Christ died for us, He forgave our sins and freed us once and for all from slavery to our destructive memories.

AN EXAMPLE OF THE ART OF FORGETTING

Perhaps Joseph, among all of our Old Testament spiritual ancestors, is the most vivid illustration of the importance of forgetting destructive events from the past. So important was the need to forget, in fact, that Joseph actually named one of his sons Manasseh, which means "The Lord has made me to forget."

Without doubt, Joseph had a good many experiences in his past that he needed to forget—and forgive. In the biblical account of his life, we first meet him as a lad of seventeen in Canaan. He was Jacob's favorite son. Out of jealousy his brothers rejected him, tried to do away with him, and finally sold him into slavery in Egypt.

As a slave, he rose to a responsible position in the household of Potiphar, the captain of Pharaoh's bodyguards. But when Joseph rejected the sexual advances of Potiphar's wife, she angrily accused him of trying to rape her. Joseph's refusal to compromise his integrity landed him in prison. But God was with him.

Without rehashing all of the drama in Joseph's prison experience, I'll simply remind you of his relationship with two fellow prisoners, Pharaoh's dismissed butler and baker. When the butler and the baker each had a dream, Joseph, with the Lord's help, told them what their dreams meant.

Much later, Pharaoh's butler, who had since been released and restored to his official position, remembered Joseph's gift for interpreting dreams. He recommended him to Pharaoh who was perplexed by two very puzzling dreams. Once again, the Lord acted through Joseph and gave him the meaning of Pharaoh's dreams.

Interpreting the dreams, Joseph explained to Egypt's ruler that the country would experience seven prosperous years of lush crops. This period would then be followed by seven years of drought and famine. Then, having interpreted the dreams, Joseph gave Pharaoh advice on what to do and how to prepare for the foretold famine. Pharaoh was so impressed by Joseph's wisdom that he made him prime minister and vice-regent over all of Egypt.

Things turned out exactly the way Joseph had predicted. And for seven years, under his leadership, Egypt stockpiled surplus grain for the future. Then famine paralyzed Egypt and the surrounding Near Eastern countries.

Back in Canaan, Joseph's father and brothers ran out of food. In danger of starvation, Jacob sent his sons to Egypt to buy supplies. Joseph, now in charge of food distribution, recognized his brothers, though they didn't recognize him.

Next follows the fascinating story of Joseph's cat-and-mouse game with his brothers, until he finally told them who he was and explained that he held no grudge against them for having sold him as a slave. This particular scene in the drama ends with Joseph, his father, and his brothers all being united again. With the Lord's help, Joseph was able to forgive his brothers and forget the evil they had done him. And because he did, they all settled in Egypt and the Hebrew nation was born.

Now, if we ourselves are to forgive, we need to assume the name Manasseh, "The Lord has made me to forget." We also need to discover how to cooperate with the Lord in this dynamic process. He will not force us against our wills. The burning question is: How can we become willing participants? How can the healing of memories take place?

TROUBLESOME MEMORIES

Here's how it has worked for me. Several years ago I realized the "left luggage" room of my memory was overloaded with three kinds of troublesome memories. First, there were memories I hoped would never be exposed; second, there were hoarded memories of failures; and, third, there were hurting memories of what others had done to me. Repeatedly, I would go into my "left luggage" room, unpack those memories, and rehash them. I reexperienced all the pain and squandered a lot of energy in this unproductive habit. It blocked my ability to remember the good things.

One day I decided I needed to receive the Lord's healing. I wanted to be free to live in the present and be hopeful about the future. I took a legal-sized sheet of paper and made a long list of the memories I needed to forget. Three headings divided the memories into categories: Secret Memories; Memories of My Failures; Memories of What Others Have Done.

As I worked, I asked the Lord to help me dredge up anything that I had consciously or unconsciously buried. Because I had not brought things before Him on a daily basis, the list was long, covering several years. It was hard, sometimes painful, work.

When the list was as complete as I could make it by being honest with myself and the Lord, I took each memory separately, went back over the event, and made a specific surrender of the memory to the Lord, claiming His forgiveness and healing. In the case of the list of hurts from others, I asked for the power to forgive. Then in a special time of commitment, telling the Lord that I would remember to forget, I burned the list. As the flames consumed the list, I sang Charles Wesley's hymn "O for a Thousand Tongues to Sing":

> Jesus, the name that charms our fears,
> That bids our sorrows cease,
> 'Tis music in the sinner's ears,
> 'Tis life, and health, and peace.
>
> He breaks the power of canceled sin,
> He sets the prisoner free,
> His blood can make the foulest clean,
> His blood availed for me.

Wesley's words about Christ wanting to break the power of canceled sin had special meaning for me. Two thousand years ago, Christ died on the cross for my failures. When I claimed His healing power for each specific memory on my list, I could experience the breaking of the binding power of what He had already forgiven.

This decisive turning point in my Christian life happened after I had been a struggling disciple for several years. Since then I've learned how important it is to keep "short accounts," that is, to pay my bills promptly to the Lord. The "memory liabilities" side of the ledger needs to be cleared each day.

But I don't always know what needs to be confessed, cleared, and forgiven. Like all of us, I have a tendency to hurry through the confession portion of my daily prayers with a sweeping, "Lord, forgive me for all my failures and mistakes." I need to be reminded often that the biblical word for *confession* in the New Testament actually refers to the act of "saying the same thing after" and "giving assent or agreement." For me, that means allowing the Lord to tell me what needs to be cleansed. Then I repeat after Him what He has exposed that needs forgiveness or healing on a daily basis before it gets stored away in my mind to trouble me in the future. The simple daily prayer, "Lord, show me what I need to confess," works won-ders. It provides a consistent cleansing of mistakes I might defensively rationalize only to find that they haunt me later.

WE BECOME WHAT WE REMEMBER

Keeping short accounts with the Lord is so crucial, because *we become what we remember.* Unresolved guilt, unconfessed failures, and unforgiven injuries make us fearful and cautious. Our obsession with negative memo-ries short-circuits positive memories and causes us to forget God's past goodness—how He enabled us to face and overcome previous difficulties.

Recently my wife and I celebrated our wedding anniversary with a din-ner at a favorite restaurant. Our conversation focused on what each of us considered to be our twelve best memories of our years together. As we remembered, we laughed and cried. It was impossible to limit our lists to only twelve memories. One good memory sparked another. We reminisced late into the night and were the last people to leave the restaurant.

The remarkable thing about that conversation was the positive impact it had on our attitude toward our present life together. We were overcome with gratitude for the blessings God had poured out over the years. That gave us new gusto for the present challenges we face. I shudder to think what would have happened if we had tried to remember the twelve most hurtful memories of our mutual failings. Thank God, those were not lurk-ing in our minds to cloud our good memories.

We've learned the hard way that we are what we remember, both individ-ually and together in our marriage. Whenever we harbor hurts, we lock each other in the prison of the past. Inadvertently, we repeat the mistakes that are dominating our memories. Likewise, keeping short accounts with each other as well as with the Lord frees us to resolve difficulties quickly. With a liberated memory, we are able to focus on our blessings; rather than compulsively repeating mistakes, we can expect a repetition of the positive memories.

REMEMBER!

It's amazing how often the Bible challenges us to remember the faithfulness of God. In the Old Testament, Israel was admonished repeatedly, "Remember your God!" And as we review the history of the acts of God in Israel's life, we are filled with awe over what He did. Remembering God's great deeds, we have new confidence about what He will do in our lives today. The psalmist's challenge to his own soul is a good reminder for us to give ourselves:

> Bless the Lord, O my soul;
> And all that is within me, bless His holy name!
> Bless the Lord, O my soul,
> And forget not all His benefits.
>
> PSALM 103:1-2

The psalmist goes on to list some of those remembered benefits: the Lord's forgiveness, healing, interventions, faithfulness, mercy, and strength in times of weakness. We, like the psalmist, have so much to remember about the consistent goodness of God.

In the Gospel account of the Last Supper, Jesus told His disciples and us, "Do this in remembrance of Me" (Lk 22:19). Throughout history, we have been prone to apply these words of Jesus only to the celebration of the Lord's Supper. But I believe Jesus' words go beyond that to include remembering what He has done for us in His death and resurrection in *every* area of life. We need to *act* in remembrance of Jesus in all we do and say.

"Remember Jesus Christ!" was Paul's watchword. Because he did remember Christ, his memories of past sins and failures were wiped out and he was free to live with expectation of continued blessing. The apostle could face his problems because he remembered Jesus Christ. Just before his death, Paul wrote to Timothy,

Remember that Jesus Christ, of the seed of David, was raised from the dead according to my gospel, for which I suffer trouble ... even to the point of chains; but the word of God is not chained. Therefore I endure all things for the sake of the elect, that they also may obtain the salvation which is in Christ Jesus with eternal glory.

2 TIMOTHY 2:8-10

Paul's phrase, "according to my gospel," leaps out of these verses. Each of us has a gospel—the good news of Christ according to our experience. It's the account of what His cross means to us and a record of what He has done in our own personal lives. The objective truth of the biblical gospel, plus our own gospel, gives us the courage to be honest about what still needs to be healed in our memories. Knowing that Christ has forgiven us must be coupled with forgiveness for ourselves and others. Does your gospel include how the Lord has healed and continues to heal your memory through the power of forgiveness?

The poet George Kenyon was depending on God to heal his hurting memories when he wrote,

> Lord, make me ...
> Dead to the voice that memory brings,
> Accusing me of many things.

FORGIVING OURSELVES

I remember several years ago talking to a man whose gospel did not include the dynamic of forgiveness for himself. He confided that he had been unfaithful to his wife and shared with me the painful remorse he felt over what he had done. The man was most fearful of being discovered. Though he had asked God to forgive him, he still feared that his reputation would be destroyed if the affair ever became public. That was unlikely. His wife had forgiven him and was not about to publish his failure. The woman with whom he'd been involved had married another man and moved to another community. Yet this man was in a panic.

"When did this affair occur?" I asked.

I was astonished when he said, "Twelve years ago." Think of it! Can you imagine twelve years of anxious days and restless nights? It was all because the final link in the experience of the perfect love, which casts out fear, had not been completed. The man had refused to forgive himself and had endured twelve years of self-inflicted torture.

Before we become too critical of this man, we need to reflect on what still lurks in our memories that still needs forgiveness. It may be more or less serious than his infidelity. The important thing is that we accept forgiveness—God's and our own. Then, if there is restitution we need to make by asking anyone else's forgiveness, we must do it immediately.

TODAY'S ACTIONS ARE TOMORROW'S MEMORIES

Because today's actions become tomorrow's memories, it's essential to take an incisive inventory of our present life. Is there anything we are hiding? Is there anything we are doing that could not stand the test of absolute honesty or moral purity? If so, we can be sure it will be added to the composite of memories that will plague us with an even greater fear of having our past exposed.

My good friend Milton Brock, an outstanding Christian businessman, told me of a decision he made years ago.

Every decision and involvement had to withstand this crucial test: Would he have the slightest concern if his actions were reported on the front page of the *Los Angeles Times*? Not a bad test for evaluating whether what we do and say today will be a good or bad memory a year from now.

Today can be the first day of building a new past. Carol discovered that five years ago. In response to a sermon I'd given on the healing of memories, she came to see me to talk about her anxiety over the past. Though Carol had been a Christian for years, she carried the memories of a painful childhood, a divorce years before that she had kept hidden from her friends, and other mistakes she had made through the years. Struggling to keep all this hidden, she was filled with fear. Her polished exterior portrayed a happy person. Inside, she was a bundle of tension. Most of all she worried about the future, terrified that it would hold nothing more than a repetition of the past.

After Carol had finished a long explanation of her deepest feelings, we talked about the power of forgiveness in healing memories. I told her how the Lord's perfect love casts out fear. I shared my own and others' experiences of forgiveness and the freedom to forgive. We talked specifically about her failures for which she needed forgiveness and people she needed to forgive. I repeated Christ's awesome promise in Revelation 3:20: "Behold, I stand at the door and knock. If anyone hears My voice and opens the door, I will come in to him and dine with him, and he with Me."

"Carol," I said, "will you open the door and invite the Lord to fill you with His Spirit and heal your memories?"

"Yes," she replied with tears streaming down her face. "I can't go on the way I am."

After we had prayed together for some time, Carol opened the door of her memory to the Lord and committed each one of her hurting, hidden memories to Him. At the end of our prayers, Carol told me she felt more at peace than ever before. Her face was radiant with joy.

I saw Carol the other day. "How are you doing with those memories?" I asked.

"Lloyd," she said, "the gnawing fear is gone! The pain has been totally removed from those haunting memories. In fact, it's difficult to remember some of them now. And no longer having to hide my past has made me sensitive to other people who are suffering from the same kind of unhealed memories. It's especially exciting to be able to tell them what the Lord can do. What great memories I have of these past five years!"

The Lord who healed Carol stands at the door of our memories and knocks persistently. He wants to enter our "left luggage" room and tag all those hurting, hidden memories: "Healed—no longer needed for the voyage!"

Chapter Five

HAVE YOU HUGGED
YOURSELF TODAY?

PRESCRIPTION 5:
What you fear in others, you first fear in yourself.
Therefore, in response to God's unqualified acceptance,
embrace yourself as worthy of your own affirmation
and encouragement.

It looks like a credit card. Same size, same plastic material. But it's probably more important for living without fear than any credit card you own. And you'll not want to leave home without it!

It's called the Hug Card. At the center there's a black square. When you hold your thumb on the square for ten seconds, you'll discover how many hugs you need. If it remains black, you need four hugs; if it turns red, you need two hugs; green indicates you need only one hug; and if it registers blue, you are ready to give a hug away to someone else.

I've had lots of fun with my family and close friends, experimenting with the Hug Card. It's a great conversation piece, and I'm especially delighted when the black square turns to blue and I get to give a hug away.

Telling you about that card may seem like a lightweight beginning to a chapter in a book on the heavyweight subject of living without fear. Not at all. We all need hugs of affirmation and affection. And more than that, we need the embrace of total acceptance.

The One Person We Need to Embrace

As I've reflected on this idea, I've come to see that we not only need the embrace of acceptance and approval from others, we are in desperate need of being able to embrace *ourselves*. But because we know so well the real person inside our own skin, most of us have that haunting feeling that we don't deserve a hug from ourselves. Our sense of self-appreciation and self-esteem is low because we don't think we measure up.

And because we're convinced deep inside that we're not very nice or that we are failures, we tend to be critical of ourselves. Even as we withhold approval from someone else whom we disagree with or dislike, we're unable to affirm ourselves, because we're sure we don't deserve it.

Instead of being "our own best friend," we become victims of a subtle but paralyzing kind of fear—fear of ourselves. No one knows our shortcomings and overlooks our struggles better than we do. We're fearful of our need always to be right, of our feelings of jealousy when a friend or colleague makes good, of our drive for prestige and power, or of our need to manipulate others to get what we want.

The other day I greeted a friend I'll call Bill with a cheery "How are you?"

He responded with surprising frankness. "I'll be OK if I can just keep Bill caged up!" Knowing Bill, I'm sure there are some great things in him that are being caged along with those things he fears about himself.

Most of us identify with Bill. Our past mistakes make us fearful about what we might do or say under pressure. Our "foot in mouth" disease causes us to worry or keeps getting us in trouble. *How could I have said that?* pops into our minds after a heated exchange. More than once at the end of a day, I've said, *Self, I warned you never to act that way, but you've gone and done it again.*

THE FRIEND INSIDE

If we treated our friends the way we treat ourselves, putting down strengths and touting mistakes, we wouldn't have any friends left. That's what happens when we get down on the person inside us. We risk losing one of the best friends we could ever have.

Abraham Lincoln said, "When I lay down the reins of this administration I want to have one friend left. And that friend is inside me."

That's a tall order. A true friend knows our strengths and helps us develop them. He also knows our weaknesses and gives us courage to face and overcome them. He is not afraid of us. That's the kind of friend we have in Jesus Christ. And I firmly believe He is eager to help us be the same kind of friend to ourselves.

Think of it this way. In the third prescription for living without fear, we claimed the biblical truth that perfect love casts out fear. Freed from guilt, we ran joyfully into the loving arms of the Father. Then, as we considered the story of Joseph, we asked God to heal the bitter memories that separate us from other people. Now we must grapple with how God's perfect love is worked out in our relationship with ourselves.

The Lord wants our love for ourselves to reflect His unconditional love. His love must heal our basic fear of ourselves. We are made in such a way that we are not truly free until we are willing to embrace ourselves as loved, cherished, and forgiven people with great potential. We need deliverance from the imprisonment we've inflicted on ourselves.

And so we must press on to the next vital prescription for living without fear: *What you fear in others, you first fear in yourself. Therefore, in response to God's unqualified acceptance, embrace yourself as worthy of your own affirmation and encouragement.*

Now, to explain this further, I want to share a moving experience I had while writing this book.

My preparation involved prolonged research into the causes and cures of fear. I carefully reviewed observations I had collected from more than forty years of talking with people about their fears. But my study of fear also included a ruthless honesty with myself about my own fears. As I worked on the prescriptions for living without fear, I tried to take each "dose of medicine" myself. This fifth prescription turned out to be one I particularly needed to assimilate.

Late one night I sat alone in my study. My desk was piled high with notes and research about fear caused by estrangement from ourselves. I began to pray about how to put into words what I had learned about this important step. I had planned to write about Allen and a few contemporary people who had discovered the power of self-acceptance and approval. I had no intention of sharing my own experiences.

That should have tipped me off. I usually avoid being personal when something I'm trying to write or preach about is needed in my own life. It's so much easier, and safer, to talk about theory and illustrate it with an anecdote from other people's lives. But who wants to hear an impersonal sermon or read a safe and cautious book?

An Unusual Exercise

As I thought about this fifth prescription, the Lord put me through an exercise that forced me to experience it in a new and fresh way. I had always thought of myself as a person with a healthy self-acceptance, problems and all. But that night I discovered a deeper level of the Lord's love for me than I had experienced in thirty-nine years of being a Christian.

Here's how it happened. After what seemed like a long time of silence, the Lord gave me a strange instruction. I didn't hear His voice audibly, but the words that He formed in my mind were impelling. *Lloyd*, the Lord said, *close your eyes. Now form in your mind's eye an image of yourself.*

I couldn't do it! The image wouldn't form in my mind. That in itself was revealing to me. How had I gotten so out of touch with myself? It had been a busy year, with an endless succession of long, exhausting days and short nights for rest.

My friend Ralph Osborne often cautions me, "Take care of Lloyd!" Had

I failed to do that? More precisely, had I been so engulfed in my projects and prayers for others that I had not allowed the Lord to care for me? On an even deeper level, had I missed keeping in touch with the Lord about my own fears and failures?

It was probably a combination of all these, and I was beginning to have a less-than-good feeling about Lloyd. I became unhappy with myself as I thought about all the things I had left undone—all the times I had been less than my best for the Lord.

I felt like J.B. Phillips who, at the height of his career in speaking, translating the Scriptures, and writing books telling Christians that their God was too small, exclaimed, "Whatever happened to Jack Phillips?"

Now the Lord showed me what had happened to Lloyd Ogilvie. I became overwhelmed with the realization that I needed a fresh experience expressed by the title of my television program: "Let God Love You!"

As I enjoyed a fresh touch of the Lord's Spirit and felt His unqualified love for me, an image of myself began to form in my mind. I no longer had to block it because of self-judgment. And what I saw was the loved, joyous person the Lord released me to picture.

Then the Lord put me to a further test. *Lloyd, go put your arms around yourself. Actually picture your "punitive-self" embracing your "struggling self."*

Lord, I responded, *that's not easy. It's so much easier to embrace and encourage others. Knowing all You and I know about Lloyd, do You still want me to embrace him? What about that improvement program we've been working on? What about the inadequacies and insufficiencies?*

Do it! the Lord commanded.

I followed orders. As I dared to embrace myself in an extension of the Lord's gracious embrace, I felt a deeper self-acceptance than ever before. A profound inner peace flooded me, followed by a new resilience and freedom. With tears streaming down my face, I sat there praising the Lord that in spite of everything, I could be a priest to myself. I could offer Christ's love, forgiveness, and acceptance to the needy person inside.

Now, I'm not suggesting that we become involved in some kind of spiritualized narcissism, an unhealthy preoccupation with the self; neither am

I recommending sloppy subjectivism. Rather, the final link in experiencing Christ-centered, cross-oriented, healing grace is to fully embrace our whole selves. Reconciliation with ourselves will give us freedom to love, not fear, ourselves. The result will be a greater willingness to allow the Lord to continue to change the very things that frighten us about ourselves. And as those changes occur, we'll be amazed at our new ability to embrace others.

All this has an authentic basis in Scripture. Let's turn our attention to one of the most personal, autobiographical passages in Paul's epistles.

HOW PAUL EMBRACED HIMSELF

In 1 Corinthians 15, Paul allows us to get inside his mind as he embraces himself as a man in Christ: "By the grace of God I am what I am, and His grace toward me was not in vain; but I labored more abundantly than they all, yet not I, but the grace of God which was with me" (v. 10).

This personal parenthesis is poignant in the midst of Paul's soaring rhetoric about Christ's death for our forgiveness; His resurrection for our victory over death; His appearances to Peter, James, the other apostles, and last of all to Paul himself. The appearance of the risen Christ was important to Paul, because it was his badge of apostleship.

But not everyone in the early church accepted that. Some questioned Paul's authority. Others differed sharply with his policy of accepting Gentile converts into the church. Paul seems to have had this criticism in mind as he wrote of his encounter with Christ, his dramatic conversion on the Damascus Road: "Then last of all He was seen by me also, as by one born out of due time. For I am the least of the apostles, who am not worthy to be called an apostle, because I persecuted the church of God" (1 Cor 15:8-9). Paul then went on to declare his grace-rooted self-acceptance, "But by the grace of God I am what I am."

I am convinced that this healthy, fearless self-acceptance in the context of the Lord's love for him explains why Paul was one of the most loving, forgiving, adventuresome, courageous human beings who ever lived. In this passage giving the progression of the apostle's experience, we discover the three elements of a Christ-motivated self-embrace.

Confessing Who We Are Apart From Grace and Accepting Grace

First, Paul shows us that embracing ourselves begins with an honest recognition of who we are apart from God's grace. He wrote frankly about that. The apostle honestly admitted that his early self-hate had manifested itself in angry persecution of the church. In describing who he had been before meeting Christ, Paul purposely used a condemnatory phrase his enemies were using against him, "one born out of due time."

There have been many different interpretations of what Paul meant by this. Some suggest he meant that, if he had been born earlier or in Galilee rather than in Tarsus, he would have responded to Jesus' ministry and become one of His disciples. But actually, Saul of Tarsus was probably a student of Gamaliel in Jerusalem at the time of Jesus' ministry, death, and resurrection. And for him to be appointed to purge the early church, he must have been a Pharisee in high authority in the Jewish leadership in Jerusalem.

I think Saul had known about Jesus of Nazareth; from an angry, judgmental distance, he had watched the events of Jesus' death and scoffed at the rumors of His resurrection. When Christ's apostles claimed Jesus was alive, Saul gladly accepted the bloody task of attacking the church, for now he had a cause to match his turbulent, hostile heart.

I think the best way to interpret Paul's identification of himself as "one born out of due time" is to stick to the literal meaning of the Greek word he used. It means "miscarriage" or "untimely birth." That Greek word is what some called him, and Paul simply accepted it. His new birth in Christ had not happened the same way as for the other apostles. Not only was it later, it was unexpected and unappreciated by some of the Christian brothers. Rather than becoming defensive, Paul could say, "Christ appeared even to me, a miscarriage." He knew that at the time Christ chose and called him, he was a kind of miscarriage in that he was destroying his birthright as a child of God. But whatever others said about Paul was nothing in comparison to what he said about the kind of person he had been before he received the Lord's grace.

Through Christ's regenerating process, Paul became a new person. During Paul's fourteen years of prayer and preparation after his conversion and before his first missionary journey, the Lord worked within his mind and heart to produce a miracle. Paul wrote about this transformation in his second letter to the Corinthian Christians: "Therefore, if anyone is in Christ, he is a new creation; old things have passed away; behold, all things have become new. Now all things are of God, who has reconciled us to Himself through Jesus Christ, and has given us the ministry of reconciliation" (2 Cor 5:17-18). That transformation gave Paul reason to put his arms around himself.

Living in Humble Praise

Knowing that "all things are of God," Paul could give humble praise for the person he had become and all that had been accomplished through him. That praise made it possible for him to say, "By the grace of God I am what I am, and His grace toward me was not in vain" (1 Cor 15:10). The grace of God in Christ had reached the depths of Paul's prior self-negation and healed him to the extent that he could take delight in the new person he'd become.

One thing is sure. We know that we have experienced the full transforming power of God's love when we can say, *By God's grace, I am what I am. It hasn't been in vain.* The Greek word Paul used for *vain* means "empty." God's grace was full and overflowing. And as part of the overflow, Paul couldn't stop praising the Lord for all He had done. To refuse to embrace the new miracle of grace inside of himself would have been paramount to blasphemy.

Let's face it. Most of us are not self-made women or men. We are what we are by God's grace alone. Knowing that does not engender pride but praise. It spurs us on, anxious to experience more grace.

Near the end of his life, Paul had that fine blend of fulfilled unfulfilled-ness. "Not that I have already attained, or am already perfected; but I press on, that I may lay hold of that for which Christ Jesus has also laid hold of me" (Phil 3:12). That's it! The more we embrace what the Lord has accomplished in us, the more we want to press on. Embracing ourselves frees us to reach out and "hug" the future.

Paul wrote in Colossians 2:18: "Let no one defraud you of your reward, taking delight in false humility." Good advice! Let's not cheat ourselves with a false humility that magnifies our weaknesses. All this does is to make us so down on ourselves that we can't praise God for the miracle He's pulling off in our characters and personalities.

This truth is beautifully illustrated by the story of the scholar Mauretis who, ill with malnutrition, was picked up along the side of the road and brought into a hospital. Two doctors consulted about what they should do with him, and both decided to just let him die because he was a "worth-less human being." Hearing what they said, he gathered the last bit of his strength, sat up in bed, and said, "Physicians, listen! Can you call anyone worthless for whom Christ died?"

A good question. What right do we have to call ourselves worthless? Or inadequate? Or insufficient? Or a failure? Christ died for us and lives in us!

As I look back over my life, God has been so good. The only word I can use to describe His goodness is that it includes many serendipities—unex-pected surprises. God has intervened to give me strength when I was weak, insight and wisdom when I had little of my own, and power when I could not generate it myself.

R.C. Sproul exemplifies this. Today he is an outstanding Christian writer. And yet when he was in the eighth grade, his classmates said, "Sproul, you can't write!" His teacher knew better. One of his papers was so remarkable that the teacher put it up on the board and said, "Don't let anyone ever say that R.C. Sproul can't write!"

Now, years later, Sproul is writing about the depths of the mysteries of

God. When he received one manuscript back from his editor, he glanced at the first page. It was full of editorial corrections. All the feelings from eighth grade came flooding back, and he said, "If the rest of the pages are like that"—and he multiplied the number of pages by the number of corrections on the first page—"then there must be ten thousand corrections in that manuscript! R.C. Sproul can't write!" But then he stopped, took a deep breath, went back over it, and asked for the Lord's blessing on his effort. When he had finished, he remembered the words of the teacher, "Don't let anyone ever say that R.C. Sproul can't write."[1]

Engaging in Heroic Service

Paul's embrace of himself as a new creation in Christ not only enabled honest confession and humble praise; it also led him to the third step of embracing himself. He became involved in heroic service. That's always the sure test of the I-am-what-I-am-by-grace embrace of self-acceptance. The last part of 1 Corinthians 15:10 states: "I labored more abundantly than they all, yet not I, but the grace of God which was with me."

And it was true. None of Paul's critics, not even the other apostles, accomplished what the Lord did through Paul's missionary journeys to Asia and Europe, Jerusalem, Ephesus, Athens, Rome—the centers of human religions, commerce, philosophy, and power. All felt the impact of a transformed Pharisee who knew Christ's embrace, embraced himself, and was free to embrace others, from the least to the mighty.

An alcoholic who has learned that I stop at a particular coffee shop some mornings on the way to my office positions himself by the door of the shop waiting for me to come by. He always needs money and some conversation. The other day he greeted me by saying, "I'm here for you!" What he meant was that he knew my schedule and was waiting for me.

But his words had a deeper meaning. In a real way, he was there for *me*. I needed to give as much as he needed to receive. And the more secure I am in the Lord's grace, the freer I am to realize that reaching out to people like that man is as important as getting to my office for a day's work.

Seven Words in Three Seconds

"I really care about what concerns you!" These seven words take only three seconds to say silently as we look into another person's eyes while we shake hands or give greetings. Those who have a deep sense of the Lord's care for them can express these words nonverbally. A few weeks ago I shared this idea at a training session for volunteer liaisons who help keep me informed of needs in their Senate offices. I have 125 of these intercessors. They seek to be sensitive to the people around them, so I suggested this method. They report that the nonverbal communication often leads to opportunities to tell people how much they care and are willing to pray and help.

I've suggested the same idea in my Senate Bible studies. The response has been enthusiastic. One staff member said, "I used to pass the desks of people in my office, greeting them but not really caring about them. I had stopped asking, 'How are you?' because I didn't want people to tell me. In the Bible study luncheon I was really convicted about my lack of empathy for my coworkers; I was overcome by God's love for me, so I tried the seven words. First I allowed the Holy Spirit to give me the gift of love coupled with discernment of people's needs. Then I started saying the seven words in my heart as I greeted people or spent time with them. My attitudes toward them changed, and it's exciting to see how people respond to me now."

Most of us respond readily to a person who is honestly interested in us. We're hungry for deep and caring relationships in which we can be wholly ourselves and talk about how to live our faith in the stresses and pressures of life.

REACHING OUT

I once had the privilege of preaching at the women's prison in Chino, California. Fr. James Fallon, a Roman Catholic priest who had become a good friend of mine, was one of the prison chaplains. Fr. Jim asked me to come and speak.

When I arrived I looked out over a roomful of women who were in desperate need of Christ's loving embrace. He was there in power as Fr. Jim led the meeting, and I talked about the cross and how to receive grace and begin a new life.

Tears streamed down their faces as they responded to the Lord's love. At the end of the service, I gave a simple invitation. All but two women stood up and came forward. It took us an hour and a half to pray for all of them.

Every so often during that hour and a half I looked over at Fr. Jim. His radiant face nodded to me; he seemed to be saying, *Go on, go on. This is the Lord's moment!*

One woman said, "I've never seen my little boy. I've been here eight years. I've got five more to go. He's going to be thirteen before I ever see him. Pray that God will take care of him. I want to become a Christian tonight."

Another woman asked for help to be able to give her life to the Lord and allow Him to love her. She'd been in prison for decades. She had never made parole, maybe because the first question the parole board always asked was "Are you repentant of the crime you committed?" And she'd say, "What crime?" But that night she said to me, "Please pray that I can receive God's love and accept His forgiveness and be honest with the parole board." After I prayed for her, I gave her a hug and thanked her for being my new sister in Christ.

On the way home, Fr. Jim said to me, "No one but the Lord could have done what happened tonight." He was right. With the Lord's arms around us, we had been used to embrace those desperate women with His love and hope.

We don't need to go to a prison to find people who are imprisoned and need our love. They are in our families, in our churches, at work, and everywhere in our communities. They need our love and encouragement.

There's a direct relationship between our daily experience of God's grace and our willingness to communicate His grace to other people. The more we accept ourselves as loved by the Lord, the more we'll be free to let go of our fear of ourselves. Pretentious pride and false humility are both unnecessary. We can say with Paul, "I am what I am by the grace of God."

God knows our failures and has forgiven us. He knows our potential and affirms us. We dare not do less for ourselves. I challenge you, by God's enabling grace: Know and confess your failures. Forgive yourself. Look ahead to discover your potential. And in faith walk toward it. Go ahead—embrace yourself!

Chapter Six

WHO CAN?
THE GIFT OF INADEQUACY

PRESCRIPTION 6:
Admit that you are inadequate to meet life's opportunities. You can conquer your fear by becoming a riverbed for the flow of God's guidance, love, and power.

I want to give you a gift.

It's one I need to receive every hour of every day. It is the gift of freedom to accept the idea that all of us are inadequate.

That's probably the last gift in the world you ever expected me to want to give you. In fact, you probably expected my gift to be one of affirmation for your talents and abilities. As you know from reading this far, I believe in affirmation, but it does contain a built-in difficulty. It tends to build up a false confidence in our own strength, and God always has a way of pressing us beyond our own capabilities.

If we only tout other people's skills or even their untapped potential, we mislead them into believing they will always have what it takes.

No one has what it takes. The truth is we are inadequate to deal with the constantly changing, ever-escalating opportunities of life. We become gripped with fear when we try to be adequate on our own, because that simply isn't possible.

In reality, our feelings of inadequacy are a blessing. They can lead us to the next giant step in overcoming unhealthy fear.

So here's the sixth prescription for living without fear: *Admit that you are inadequate to meet life's opportunities. You can conquer your fear by becoming a riverbed for the flow of God's guidance, love, and power.*

A TURNING POINT

How does this life-changing prescription work?

A few years ago, a man came to see me to discuss his fear of being inadequate to handle the many personal and professional problems that were confronting him.

"Up until now," Robert said, "I've been able to take life in stride. I've never felt inadequate to step up to bat and hit the ball out of the park, so to speak. But now I've been given more responsibilities at work. At the same time, one of my sons is in real trouble. I've used all the self-affirmation and thought-conditioners I know for developing a positive attitude.

"I stand before the mirror when I shave in the morning and say, 'Robert, you can do it; you've got what it takes, so believe in yourself. You've been a skyrocketing success at work and a model father. You can win, Tiger, you can win!'

"But by the end of the day, I realize that the pep talk didn't work. I really fear messing up at work, and my boy has me on the ropes. For the first time in my life, I really feel inadequate."

"Perhaps you are inadequate," I said quietly, with a feeling of empathy.

Robert was stunned. He looked at me intently, disappointment and shock written all over his face. He looked like I'd just punched him in the stomach with a hard jab.

"What do you mean?" He was indignant. "I came to see you to get a lift, not have my worst fear confirmed. I needed you to cheer me up, not put me down."

At the very least, I had Robert's attention.

"My friend," I said, "you are on the edge of making one of life's most crucial discoveries. You are ready for a liftoff to a new level of life. You know that you are a talented and highly trained professional. And we both know how much you love your kids. In both areas you are being pressed with challenges where you are inadequate—by yourself. You need God's help.

"He's ready to use abilities you don't know you have and multiply your efforts with the gifts of wisdom, vision, and power only He can provide. The feeling of inadequacy can either be a source of discouragement or the beginning of new courage. You don't have all that's needed for this time in your life, but God does. And He wants to help you."

At that time, Robert was one of those Christians with a vague faith. Now, for the first time, he was up against difficulties beyond his human resources.

We talked at length about how Christ wanted to live in him and give him supernatural power. We discussed the great things Christ had done through people who depended on Him. Not only were their own abilities expanded, but they were also given discernment, insight, ideas, solutions, and inventive genius beyond anything they could have produced on their own.

Then I shared with Robert the secret of how to receive that supernatural power: (1) a total surrender of our challenges; (2) an invitation for Christ to live in us; (3) an intimate, dependent relationship with Him; and (4) a willingness to give God the glory when we perform beyond our human adequacy.

We ended our discussion with prayer. Robert confessed his inadequacy and asked the Lord to fill him with superhuman adequacy. And with love and power Christ came into Robert's life. Day by day, as he began to rely on the Lord's adequacy, Robert received the wisdom and strength he needed for his challenges at work and with his family.

That turning point in Robert's life took place several years ago. Since then he's faced bigger and more demanding opportunities at work than he ever thought would be entrusted to him. And the challenges at home and in the rest of his life haven't stopped either. Each new challenge keeps him on the edge of new growth in Christ.

Just recently when I ran into Robert, he said, "Life doesn't get easier, but it sure does get more exciting. The moment I get comfortably settled on a plateau thinking I can handle things myself again, I get pushed into some new responsibility beyond what I can tackle alone. The great thing is that the bigger the problem or the chance to try something really innovative and creative, the more strength and skill I'm given. The hardest part is remembering to let everyone around me know that the Lord gets the glory. Don't ever let me forget that!"

"I won't," I replied with a smile. "And don't let me forget it either."

We've become brothers in that pact. It's encouraging to have a friendship in which we both can admit our fear of inadequacy and remind each other that Christ is going to keep pushing us beyond our abilities so that we can be riverbeds for the flow of more of His power through us.

KEEPING LIFE PARED DOWN

I'm sure you've heard of the Peter Principle: the theory that people rise in life to the level of their incompetence. Certainly, that's true for lots of people who rise to a level beyond their abilities and bungle the new opportunities they are given. In a similar vein, here is what might be called an Ogilvie Principle: As Christians, we should constantly be rising to the level of our human inadequacy, for only then can we discover the amazing gift of Christ's adequacy.

Unfortunately, many Christians fall into a crippling trap. They rise to the level of their inadequacy and are gripped with the fear of being inadequate. Instead of receiving Christ's power to make them adequate, they are filled with panic about not having what some relationship or responsibility requires.

In response to that panic, many of us keep life pared down to our human limitations. "I'd never be able to do *that!*" we exclaim. Or, "You'll never catch me attempting that. I'd fall on my face." Or, "Leave the heroics to someone else. I'll stick to what I'm sure I can do on my own."

That attitude is deadly and life paralyzing. We settle for a supine smallness of vision.

But it doesn't work for long. The moment we think we have life narrowed down to what we can handle, we are confronted with unexpected intrusions into our constricted little world.

It is true that we all have problems that make us feel inadequate. And we can be sure that when these are solved, there will be others, probably bigger ones than we ever thought we would have to wrestle with. The Lord will always give us more to do and more to attempt for Him than we can ever handle alone. But we can also be sure that God will give us the ability to meet every challenge He places before us.

I'm convinced that unless we are attempting something we could not pull off on our own strength, we have surrendered to the fear of being inadequate. As a result, we become timid and shrink back from attempting what we are called to do. We refuse to take the next step in our spiritual growth.

My Own Experience

The fear of inadequacy haunted me through many years as a younger man. The longing to be adequate became a false god for me through the early years of my Christian life. Rooted in feelings of inadequacy from my youth, it carried over into my Christian experience.

Accomplishments, degrees, and recognition did little to feed my voracious hunger to be recognized as an adequate person. The therapy that was a part of my training as a pastoral counselor helped me see that the causes for my feelings were rooted in certain family and adolescent experiences. But that self-understanding did little to offset the feeling that some day people would discover how inadequate I really was. I tried to hide my fear behind a highly polished exterior of adequacy. But that became a barrier to deep relationships with people and kept me from discovering the secret of freedom in Christ.

This scenario occurred early in my ministry, when I faced opportunities that exceeded my human capabilities, and I knew I could not make it on my own. Finally, when I confronted this honestly, the Lord gave me a three-part gift to help me admit my inadequacy and receive His power.

A Lesson From My Heroes

The first part of the gift opened my eyes to a most important truth that had eluded me. Everywhere I turned in my Bible study and while reading the biographies of great Christian leaders, I was struck by a common theme. Encounters with Christ spurred them on to attempt the impossible. The Lord constantly pressed them beyond their human capabilities. In the dangerous interface between what they were and what He called them to be, they discovered His power. And in drawing on that power, they persistently took risks with raw faith. The greater the risk, the more faith and daring they received.

I began to see that by trying to become adequate I was cutting myself off not only from the flow of the Lord's power, but from the humanly impossible things He wanted to do through me.

No Time to Relax

The second part of the Lord's gift helped me realize that I will never be able to rest easy at any level of growth. It became obvious that every accomplishment in my life had been followed by some new challenge that was far beyond my own human ability to face and solve. I never had time to sit back and savor success. New and fresh challenges always kept me aware of my inability to cope without the Lord's intervention and strength. It was a great relief to accept, finally, that this is the way it's always going to be. Right up to the last day of my physical life!

The Fellowship of the Inadequate

The third part of the gift came in what I call the fellowship of the inade-quate. The Lord gave me a group of people with whom I met each week. We studied the Bible, shared our needs, and prayed for each other. Every person in the group was highly successful in some area, and yet all felt this same sense of being inadequate for the challenges entrusted to them. The Lord had arranged for people with a common need to be my fellow-adven-turers.

The group galvanized into oneness. The Lord consistently gave us awe-some challenges that forced us to realize that we were inadequate without Him and that we needed each other's support and prayers. Each time one of us would come close to victory over some soul-sized problem, someone would say, "Now that the Lord's won that battle, get ready for the next one!" And sure enough, usually in the next week or two, some opportu-nity would develop to convince us of our inadequacy and His amazing ade-quacy for our needs. This was a great learning and growing experience for me, because I learned never to trust myself to attempt the adventure with-out Christ.

TIMOTHY AND THE SPIRIT OF FEAR

We have a colorful example in the New Testament of how the apostle Paul helped Timothy to overcome feelings of inadequacy, so he could move on to accomplish what the Lord had called him to do. In fact, the second let-ter to Timothy was sent to encourage and inspire the youth to rise above his feelings.

Young Timothy, as you may remember, was converted to Christ when Paul visited his hometown of Lystra on the first missionary journey. When Paul was in Lystra on his second missionary journey, he enlisted Timothy to be a fellow worker as he moved around Galatia, Macedonia, Greece, and the Roman province of Asia, which is today part of Turkey. Eventually,

Timothy was left in charge of the church at Ephesus.

This was not an easy assignment, because Ephesus was a "vanity fair" of pagan worship, secularism, and hostility to Christ and His followers. Trying to guide this group of new Christians was a severe test for Timothy, as he faced difficulties that far exceeded his human abilities.

Timothy may have had a lifelong struggle with feelings of inadequacy. These feelings may have been nurtured by the fact that he was naturally timid and not physically strong. At any rate, it is apparent that the Ephesian challenge had Timothy "on the ropes" when Paul spoke to his young friend's need for courage in the second letter. What we have here is kind of a last will and testament to Christian courage. A close look at Paul's advice to Timothy will be helpful for us.

Paul didn't try to cheer Timothy with easy reassurances of the young disciple's human talents and strengths. Instead, the apostle reminded him of what the Lord had done in his life, and of what the Lord would continue to do that would more than meet Timothy's feelings of inadequacy.

But Paul wanted Timothy to do something in preparation to receive the Lord's gift: "I remind you to stir up the gift of God which is in you through the laying on of my hands" (2 Tm 1:6). What was this gift Timothy had received that Paul wanted him to stir up? It was the greatest gift of all—the indwelling Spirit of the living Christ. This is the same gift Paul encouraged the Galatian Christians to claim, "Because you are sons, God has sent forth the Spirit of His Son into your hearts" (Gal 4:6).

The Spirit of Christ had set a fire of vision and conviction burning in Timothy. Fellowship with Paul, Silas, and Luke had kept that flame ablaze as they had traveled together and encouraged each other in the ministry of evangelism. Now, alone in leadership in Ephesus, Timothy needed to rekindle Christ's fire within him. Paul didn't tell him to try harder or pray longer. Rather, Paul told him to return to the source of his supernatural strength.

STIRRING UP THE FIRE

Paul's advice to Timothy applies to us, because we need to be on-fire Christians. We may have allowed the fire of Christ's Spirit to become smothered with neglect or resistance. Our fire may have fizzled out because we have tried to be faithful disciples on our own strength. We may have tried to run on our own resources without being fueled by constant dependence on the Lord. We may have even tried to live the Christian life without Christ!

The only cure is to stir up the banked fires within us. Clarence Jordan translates Paul's admonition in a vivid way, "I'm reminding you to shake the ashes off the God-given fire that's in you." In other words, shake the grate until the embers are exposed, use the poker to push the coals together, and then use the bellows to blow them into flaming life. That's exactly what we do when we can't face a challenge or responsibility and cry out for Christ to refuel the fire within us with a fresh inflow of His Spirit.

GOD IS NOT THE SOURCE OF FEAR

Paul next reminds Timothy that God is not the source of fear that comes from feelings of timidity or inadequacy: "God has not given us a spirit of fear" (2 Tm 1:7). This particular Greek word for *fear* is *deilia*, a word that is always used in a bad sense for cowardice or timidity. And why do we so often have feelings like those? We don't think we have what it will take to confront and handle life's soul-stretching problems; we feel inadequate to cope.

The word *spirit*, as it is used in verse 7, means "a pervading mood, attitude, and mode of thinking." In other words, the spirit of fear cripples us with caution and reserve. It limits what we are willing to attempt to only those things we are sure we can do on our own strength. We get all wrapped up in ourselves—usually a very small package!

Capitol Hill has its own brand of this type of fear. Political leaders often feel the need to establish an image of adequacy to get elected and stay in office. In fact, some political campaigns have become attacks on the opponent's character and qualifications for office. Millions of dollars are spent in television ads to denigrate political opponents. All this makes leaders very defensive. It's easy to boil a hard shell around a very insecure person inside. The pattern of pretended adequacy carries over to the term of office and results in a lack of freedom to admit needs and allow the Lord and fellow believers to offer encouragement and attention. This is why it is so important to have "safe places," small sharing groups in which trust can be established and people can dare to admit their needs. Fear of appearing inadequate is overcome only by an honest admission that we'll always be insufficient to meet the mounting challenges of life. That honesty opens us to receive courage and strength from God as well as the help of others. We were never meant to make it on our own!

Paul makes it clear to his young friend that the kind of fear he's talking about does not come from God. This kind of fear is brought on by feelings of inadequacy that straitjacket the creativity and freedom of God's Spirit. And, unfortunately, the deadly fear of inadequacy locks us into the level of inadequacy. On the other hand, if we turn that fear over to the Lord and let Him heal it, we are released to attempt the great things He wants us to do.

Paul follows up by saying that the indwelling Spirit of Christ gives us a spirit of "power and of love and of a sound mind" (v. 7). Because Paul often puts the key word in a list last, I'd like to review the Spirit's supernatural adequacy in us by considering these gifts in the order that they are usually given in our experience. A sound mind precedes the ability to love, and the commitment to love leads us to ask for spiritual power.

The Spirit of a Sound Mind
The first of the Spirit's gifts is a "sound mind." The Greek word used here is descriptive of a Spirit-anointed, disciplined mind, one totally under the

control of the Spirit of Christ. It is a mind able to think like Christ and see the potential of people and situations the way He does. In a sound mind, the powers of imagination are whole and healthy. With a sound mind, the Christian focuses on the Lord's vision for specific opportunities in life.

To put it another way, a sound mind overcomes fears of inadequacy with a Spirit-produced attitude toward challenges and the resources we need and will be given to face them. A Christ-inspired, sound mind provides reliable guidance and clear vision. It lifts our focus beyond what we can do on our own strength to what the Lord wants to do through us.

Let's face it. We need the Lord's help in every relationship, situation, and problem where life dishes out challenges beyond us. Wherever we feel inadequate—in marriage, with our families, on the job, in our opportunities to share our faith, and in the impossible tasks the Lord has given us to do—we need to confess, *Lord, I can't make it on my own; this is beyond me; I just don't have what it takes!*

To such a prayer, I believe His response would be: *Good, you were never meant to be adequate on your own. Now, relax and allow Me to think through your mind, and I'll reveal My strategy and show you how you will accomplish it with My strength.*

We don't have to thrash about with uncertainty. The Lord will guide and provide.

The Spirit of Love

A sound mind is able to conceive and transmit to our emotions the assurance that we are loved by the Lord. We not only know we are loved by the Lord, but we also *feel* loved. His Spirit of love flows into and through us. Most of life's challenges that make us feel inadequate are those in which we are called to love beyond our human ability. Think of the people whom you find difficult to love as much as they need to be loved. Reflect on the people who have hurt you and whom you also find impossible to forgive. Focus on the people who demand more of your time and resources than you feel capable of giving. Or consider the situations in which you need to give yourself sacrificially and want to pull back. Again, you may protest, *It's too much, Lord! The needs of people are greater than I can meet!*

And yet the great need in the world is for Christians with passion. Passion is Christ's intense love burning in us for people and human suffering. John Henry Jowett, a great preacher of a past generation, wrote, "The gospel of the broken heart demands the ministry of bleeding hearts ... as soon as we cease to bleed, we cease to bless ... we can never heal the needs we do not feel. Tearless hearts can never be the heralds of Christ's passion."[1]

A passion for the needs of people—a broken and bleeding heart—really makes us feel inadequate. To see suffering and realize what love demands creates the most desperate sense of insufficiency. That's why a sound mind, capable of thinking with the Savior and feeling with His heart the need for love for the people around us, leads us to accept the third gift Paul listed for Timothy in his antidote to the fear of inadequacy.

The Spirit of Power

Paul says that the Christian is to have not only the Spirit of a sound mind and the Spirit of love but also the Spirit of power. The Greek word used here for *power* is the root from which our word *dynamite* comes, an enabling and dynamic power. We can be assured that the Lord never calls us to do anything for which He is not willing to provide the power. In other words, it isn't that "we are able!" but "the Lord is able!" And what He is able to do for us exceeds our wildest dreams.

Paul underlined this point clearly to the Ephesian Christians: "Now to Him who is able to do exceedingly abundantly above all that we ask or think, according to the power that works in us, to Him be glory in the church by Christ Jesus throughout all ages, world without end. Amen" (Eph 3:20-21).

The key phrase for us here is "according to the power that works in us." As we experience that power and learn to depend on it, we will be free from the feeling of inadequacy.

But there's more. Receiving the power of the Spirit not only multiplies the effectiveness of our human faculties; it also gives us supernatural abilities. We are given understanding *beyond* our intellectual capabilities, love *beyond* our natural love, strength *beyond* our energies. It's what Christ does through us, not what we are able to do for Him, that accomplishes lasting results.

FRESH EACH MORNING

I had ample opportunity to rediscover the Lord's adequacy each morning during the impeachment trial of President Clinton. My responsibility was to open each day's deliberations with prayer. As sessions opened at noon, I had the morning to draft my prayers. Early each morning I would sit praying about the prayer for that day. I wanted to reaffirm that God is the Sovereign of our nation, that He guides leaders who trust in Him, and that He would bring us through the trauma and to a place where we could claim His supernatural gifts of wisdom, discernment, and vision. There had to be a balance between God's judgment and His grace. I wanted to pray for God's absolutes in the commandments without being absolutistic in tone or attitude. Keeping the parties working together was not easy. The sessions were long and physically exhausting. My prayers needed to express empathy for the senators and the president.

You can imagine I felt inadequate each morning. I wanted to be on target for what had taken place the day before and what was anticipated in the day ahead—all in a two-minute prayer that would be recorded in the *Congressional Record* and listened to by millions across the land. No wonder my preparation began with a cry for God's help. And He was faithful. In a new way I experienced Lamentations 3:22-23:

> Through the Lord's mercies we are not consumed,
> Because His compassions fail not.
> They are new every morning;
> Great is Your faithfulness.

I was given the words to pray each day. It was as if the Lord guided my pen and the words flowed.

During the long hours sitting in the Senate chamber each day, I became aware of the Lord's Spirit giving me physical strength to heal my physical weariness. I spent periods of time on both the Republican and Democratic sides of the chamber to affirm my nonpartisan role. Profound discussions with senators of both parties about moral, ethical, and spiritual issues took place in most every break in the proceedings and often late into the evenings after the daily adjournment. As the stress of the trial and the media pressures escalated, I prayed for the Lord's equipoise, the perfect inflow of His peace and outgo of confidence and trust in Him.

I'm so glad that the challenges of being Senate chaplain came after forty years of learning how to receive the gift of inadequacy and to receive the Lord's totally adequate resources for life's demanding times.

When we face the great opportunities the Lord arranges, it's not the feeling of inadequacy that's wrong but the fear of being inadequate that's rooted in a desire to be sufficient on our own. And because the challenges keep getting bigger, the luxury of always being adequate is not for us to enjoy. What we can enjoy is the assurance that the Lord will release His power in spectacular ways that are best for everybody concerned.

HUMANLY INADEQUATE, DIVINELY EMPOWERED

As the Senate chaplain, I have the privilege of meeting with the leaders of our nation on a regular basis. The intense pace of a leader's life and the weighty issues that they grapple with are enough to overwhelm anyone. But as I speak with those leaders who are part of our Bible studies and prayer groups, they recount to me their experiences of liberation. Whenever the load is too burdensome, the issues too complex, and the anxiety-producing problems are beyond their personal power to solve, the quiet voice of the Holy Spirit leads them to depend on Christ's power to do the grand work of governing. Many of these leaders exemplify the eight-word motto of my ministry to the Senate family: "Without God We Can't, Without Us He Won't."

In small towns or big cities, among the poor or the privileged, I see the spirit of fear that has taken hold of people's lives. It shows up in a devotion to the past and in an inordinate love for traditions. The spirit of fear, masquerading as a sense of inadequacy, can invade our minds when we least expect it. It tries to hold us back when we deal with the need for love in our families, face the challenges of living courageously, or become involved in the social needs of our communities.

We've spent a lot of time discussing the potentially debilitating effects of fear and praying to be given a sound mind, love, and power. What a difference that can make in our lives! And it will radically revolutionize our relationships as well!

My prayer is that you will accept the gift offered at the opening of this chapter—the gift of accepting that you are inadequate, especially in the light of the Lord's mysterious way of trusting us with ever-increasing challenges.

There's a liberating alternative to the *fear of inadequacy*. Simply admit that you are inadequate, confess the spirit of fear, and allow the Lord to become your adequacy as He fills your mind with His guidance, your heart with His love, and your life with His power!

Chapter Seven

YOU THINK
YOU'VE GOT ENEMIES?

PRESCRIPTION 7:

You are secure in God's love. Do not surrender your self-worth to the opinions and judgments of others. When you are rejected, do not retaliate; when you are hurt, allow God to heal you. And knowing the pain of rejection, seek to love those who suffer from its anguish.

It hurts. We try to pretend it doesn't matter, but it does. When we say, "I couldn't care less," we often mean, "I wish I didn't care so much!" No matter how we try to explain it away or depreciate the source, being rejected by people causes excruciating pain.

And rejection does something else. It causes fear. Memories of past rejections make us leery, cautious, and restrained. We flinch with fear for what people might do or say to hurt us. Sometimes the last thing we want is to get close to anyone. Why should we put ourselves in a vulnerable position and risk being hurt again?

When we are hurt by rejection, we are tempted to slink off alone like a wounded animal to lick our wounds. As the Scottish poet Robert Burns wrote, "I lie me doon ta grieve a while." We become aloof, strained, and fearful, not only with the people who have hurt us but with just about everyone.

We hear a lot about phobias these days. Here's one to add to the list: *apodokimophobia,* the dread of rejection. And that's one phobia from which we all suffer at times. For some of us, the fear of rejection is constantly present.

The fear of rejection not only keeps us from deep relationships; it often robs us of courage. We become solicitous and compliant. Eventually, like a chameleon, we try to blend into the background with other people's values and attitudes.

Let's face it. We all need approval and acceptance. Often we are willing to do almost anything to keep a steady flow of both coming our way. We hedge our convictions and adjust our values in order to avoid saying anything that will cause people to reject us. The result is that we need people far too much. The passion to be liked ends in panic over the possibility of being rejected.

REJECTION CAN START EARLY

Rejection starts early in life. Nearly all of us have painful memories of rejection during our growing-up years. Few have escaped.

For some it began with an aching suspicion that their parents favored one sibling over another. Others, who didn't battle with the tensions of sibling rivalry, still may not have experienced much esteem-building affirmation from their parents.

Many felt rejected when they did not "measure up" athletically. It was painful to be the last one chosen for a ball team or not chosen at all. Think of the times you were not accepted by the "in" group of kids in the neighborhood or at school. I can remember my first infatuation and the pain of discovering that my "heartthrob" didn't even know I existed.

Who can forget the longing to be popular? Maybe there were times you stood with wallflower anticipation at a school dance or wondered if you would have a date for the prom?

Added to all this may have been the fear of failure in school and the sense of rejection when you didn't quite make the grade. Pressure from parents or competition from peers can make a poor grade seem like a rejection slip from life.

MORE THAN KIDS' STUFF

Rejection is just kids' stuff? Hardly. Some of us still remember the anguish of opening college rejection letters and questioning our worth and future hopes. Few of us were accepted into the programs of our first choice. Others who never made it to college, or didn't finish, often carry a self-imposed stigma. Those of us who did make it through to graduation found the college years filled with the same pressure to be accepted and the continuing fear of rejection that we experienced as adolescents.

As adults we continue to face rejection; the only difference is that the stakes are higher. Now acceptance is essential to our success on the job. The hidden scars from growing up make many of us uneasy. Being bypassed for a long-anticipated promotion or losing a position only adds to the fear of future failure. Even the very successful tell me they worry about staying on top.

Then, too, marriage offers no guarantee of acceptance and affirmation. In fact, some of the most painful experiences of rejection can happen between husbands and wives. Constant criticisms, withheld affection, and lack of encouragement cause many a spouse to feel put off or put down.

Those who go through the trauma of divorce often feel unwanted and emotionally battered. As Rebecca, a middle-aged friend who had just received her divorce papers, explained, "I feel totally rejected. I feel like an orange with all the juice squeezed out. The best years of my life are gone, and all that's left is a broken heart and shattered dreams."

Many who are single carry the inner burden of feeling rejected. Society does little to change that self-judgment. The high priority we place on marriage often makes single people question their desirability, their attractiveness, even their sexuality.

Whether we're married or single, successful or struggling, we all experience the painful blows of rejection at one time or another. Who hasn't felt the heartache of being rejected by a loved one or friend? What they say to us or about us sets us reeling; what they *do* to hurt us sends us to the mat. We lie low for fear of further blows to the ego.

THE NEED TO BELONG

Rejection by a group is no less painful. It stirs unhealed memories of times when we didn't feel included in an inner circle of friends, or when some club or organization did not accept us. All of us long to belong. And the more important the group is to us, the more determined we are to get in and achieve solid acceptance. Our self-esteem is often based on the friends we've acquired or the prestigious groups to which we belong. When we are excluded or ignored, we feel the piercing jab of rejection.

The church is no exception. Denominations and local congregations have theological emphases and power structures. Acceptance is often reserved for those who toe the hard line. Clique words, jargon, and familiar phrases identify us as variously acceptable to the liberal, the evangelical, the charismatic, or the traditionalist. People who don't speak our language or espouse our brand of religion are excluded, even ridiculed. False pride is mingled with fictitious assurance.

Somerset Maugham put it this way in *The Moon and Sixpence:* "It is not difficult to be unconventional in the eyes of the world when your unconventionality is but the convention of your set. It affords you then an inordinate amount of self-esteem. You have the self-satisfaction of courage without the inconvenience of danger."[1]

That accurately describes the reason for factions in contemporary

Christianity. It also explains why we feel rejected by religious people who think we don't meet their standards. All too often such rejection is communicated with an assumed authority of the voice of God.

Of all the rejections of life, perhaps the most difficult to bear is the rejection expressed in people's criticisms and judgments when we fail. When we most need help to face some mistake and learn from it, we feel condemnation rather than understanding and encouragement.

A Liberating Perspective

You may be slinking in the shadows of rejection right now, lost in the darkness of discouragement and fear. But be sure of this: The Lord can deliver you. Just open your eyes to His teaching. Be open to the possibilities in this next vital prescription for living without fear of rejection: *You are secure in God's love. Do not surrender your self-worth to the opinions and judgments of others. When you are rejected, do not retaliate; when you are hurt, allow God to heal you. And knowing the pain of rejection, seek to love those who suffer from its anguish.*

This may seem like a momentous task. It will mean breaking lifelong patterns and letting go of false securities. The fear of rejection is rooted in our profound need to be loved and the false idea that other people ought to love us as much as we need to be loved. But only God can meet that aching need.

Over the years Psalm 27 has helped me overcome times of rejection. It has also been a powerful guide in helping others when fear of rejection kept them from living courageously.

In this psalm the writer shows us how to gain a liberating perspective, receive power, and experience peace. We discover from him how to pray when we feel the blows of rejection. The psalmist's panic over his enemies led him to a great conviction. He did not internalize the criticism or hostility of others; nor did he fuel the fires of fear with self-negation or self-blame. His first thought was of God and his own need for Him. Note verse 1:

> The Lord is my light and my salvation;
> Whom shall I fear?
> The Lord is the strength of my life;
> Of whom shall I be afraid?

That's exactly what we need to affirm when we feel rejected. We need the perspective that comes from the illuminating light of the Lord. In that revealing light we can see things as they really are. We can ask ourselves, *Why am I so troubled by this rebuff? Why has this person or group's opinion of me become so important? Could it be that what they think is more important to me than what God thinks? Do I need their acceptance more than His?*

IN THE SPOTLIGHT

When the light of the Lord reaches into the dark corners of our memories, we are able to see how unhealed past hurts have made us vulnerable to current rejections. We realize that without God's help, we will continue to be victimized by people's attitudes and reactions to us.

The painful experience of rejection actually becomes a blessing when it forces us to see that the fear of rejection has more power over us than God's power at work in us. That realization leads us to confess the false god we've made of people's approval and to pray for profound inner healing.

When we've reached this point we are ready, with the Lord's help, to take a close look at ourselves and what might cause others to reject us. Assured of the Lord's love, we can see ourselves as we are, asking ourselves, "Is there any truth in what people have said? Are there any eccentricities in me that would cause people to react to me the way they have? Was the criticism justified?

An honest inventory of this kind is liberating. It frees us to take responsibility for our actions. Maybe it's time to get rid of that irritating habit or think twice before making a complaint. Maybe it's time to learn to say please and thank you.

A more intense inventory may reveal that you're setting yourself up for rejection by insisting on doing or saying things that cause it.

Sometimes we actually set ourselves up for rejection. Allison, a musically gifted seminary graduate, has battled against fear and expectation of rejection for much of her life. She attributes some of her problems to family dynamics in childhood. "In some ways I always expected failure and rejection," she says. I'll let Allison tell her story in her own words:

I was excited when I was called to a small southern congregation in our denomination to serve as activity and music director. But I met with opposition at every turn. There were deep issues involved that didn't have anything to do with me, but I felt caught in the middle and felt rejected in every way. I finally left.

Other career opportunities and even my relationships with others did not measure up to my expectations. I'm sure I began to project the attitude "You probably won't want me anyway." And in most cases I received what I feared.

It took a lot of courage—and the light of the Lord—for Allison to see this pattern.

Sometimes an honest self-inventory leads to another conclusion: that in many instances we are not to blame and that the rejection is or has been unfair and unjustified. What are we to do in such a case?

WHAT'S GOING ON HERE?

When we think someone has been unjustly critical of us, we can let the illuminating light of the Lord help us to see with new eyes the people who have hurt us. Then we can ask with empathy, *What needs in this person caused him or her to reject me in this way? What insecurity, combative competitiveness, envy, or experience of rejection by others lurks behind what has been said or done to me?*

Unjust criticism or hostile rejection nearly always says more about the one doing the rejecting than about those who are rejected. Lack of love, sensitivity, and caring is what causes a person to give up on others. Manipulative rejection is a final effort to play God.

In the light of God, we can see the real power at work behind people's hostile words and actions. Satan is always ready to attack those who are trying to put God first in their lives. He uses people's rejections to influence us to question our self-worth and our status as God's chosen, called, and cherished people. Repeated experiences of rejection eventually put us in a spiritual battle with the forces of evil that are seeking to immobilize us in fear. But the Lord is infinitely greater than Satan's crafty, demeaning designs on us.

DELIVERANCE!

The good thing about knowing the real enemy is that we can cry out for the Lord's protection and victory. We can say the courage-engendering, fear-dispelling words: "The Lord is my light *and my salvation.*" For the psalmist, salvation meant deliverance from his problems and enemies. It means that for us, too, and so much more.

For us, the word *salvation* is drenched with New Testament grace and power. Emmanuel, God With Us, Christ the Lord is our salvation. In Christ's life—His message, death, and resurrection—and present power, we discover how to overcome the fear of rejection. He is able to help us because He Himself endured the full force of rejection and overcame it.

An Old Testament prophecy of the Messiah's rejection came true in Christ's life: "He is despised and rejected by men, a Man of sorrows and acquainted with grief" (Is 53:3). Jesus was rejected by the leaders of Israel, misunderstood by His family, and denied and betrayed by His disciples. Yet throughout His life, He revealed Love incarnate.

With divine authority Jesus declared a new way to deal with rejection: "You have heard that it was said, 'You shall love your neighbor and hate your enemy.' But I say to you, love your enemies, bless those who curse you, do good to those who hate you, and pray for those who spitefully use you and persecute you" (Mt 5:43-44). The words have an awesome ring in the light of our discussion of rejection. Who can live that quality of love? No one! Except by Christ's power.

THE SECRET OF LOVING OUR ENEMIES

Later in His ministry, Christ revealed the secret of His power to love His enemies. Anticipating His victory over evil and death on the cross, He said, "In the world you will have tribulation; but be of good cheer, I have overcome the world" (Jn 16:33). And indeed He did! He rose from the dead and lives as our ever-present Lord to make us overcomers when we are hit with blows of rejection.

When we invite Christ to live in us, He gives us the power to love our enemies. It is impossible to do it without Him. The sure sign that we have experienced His salvation is that we can love, bless, do good to, and pray for the very people who reject us.

And so we can affirm with the psalmist, but with Christ's Galilean accent, "The Lord is the strength of my life; / Of whom shall I be afraid?" The word *strength* used here in Psalm 27:1 can also be translated "stronghold," a place to take our stand in battle. Battling against the fear of rejection, we need both a stronghold and strength. We don't have to retreat any further. The Lord wants to heal our panic. The realization of our need is only a reflection of the Lord's greater desire to help us.

Reading further in Psalm 27, we see that the psalmist's troubles reminded him of his loneliness for God:

> One thing I have desired of the Lord,
> That will I seek:
> That I may dwell in the house of the Lord
> All the days of my life,
> To behold the beauty of the Lord,
> And to inquire in His temple.
> For in the time of trouble
> He shall hide me in His pavilion;
> In the secret place of His tabernacle
> He shall hide me;
> He shall set me high upon a rock.
>
> VERSES 4-5

Here the psalmist is not talking about a physical refuge. The shelter he describes is not an edifice but a relationship. He didn't want a cloistered life away from reality, but he knew that an intimate communion with God would bring inner tranquillity. He longed to be in the presence of the Lord. Experience had taught the psalmist that God alone could steady his nerves and cool his overheated panic.

THE LORD'S INVITATION

Like the psalmist, our desire to turn to the Lord when we are troubled is our response to His prior invitation: "Seek My face." With the psalmist we cry out to God,

Hear, O Lord, when I cry with my voice!
Have mercy also upon me, and answer me.
When You said, "Seek My face,"
My heart said to You, "Your face, Lord, I will seek."

PSALM 27:7-8

In Hebrew, the same word means both "face" and "presence." The Lord promised Moses that the Lord's face, His presence, would go with Moses and the people of Israel (Ex 33:14). Moses' response was that he would never consider pressing on without the Lord. "If Your Presence [face] does not go with us, do not bring us up from here" (v. 15). In other words, Moses said, "It's unthinkable to attempt anything without the assurance that You are with us!"

In times of rejection, the Lord says to us, "Seek My face, come to Me with your brokenness." Even before we cry out for His help, He is waiting to love us. God's promise to Israel through Isaiah gives us assurance that He is more ready to help us than we may have been ready to ask.

It shall come to pass
That before they call, I will answer;
And while they are still speaking, I will hear.

ISAIAH 65:24

Our desire to talk with the Lord comes from Him. He gives us the courage to ask for what He is ready to give. He knows exactly what we need, and our greatest need, beneath all our surface needs, is to know that He will never reject us. That alone can rebuild our confidence and courage.

When the Lord says, "Seek My face," we can be sure that He is ready to heal our wounds of rejection. In Christ we behold God's face. "For it is the God who commanded light to shine out of darkness, who has shone in our hearts to give the light of the knowledge of the glory of God in the face of Jesus Christ" (2 Cor 4:6). He reminds us of His love for us, love that prompted Him to die on the cross.

Tenderly, the ever-present Savior says to us, *You are hurting and I understand. But do not put your trust in people's attitudes and opinions. Trust only in Me. I know all there is to know about your strengths and weaknesses, and I will never give up on you. I will comfort you.*

THE KING KNOWS

Amy Carmichael, missionary to India a couple of generations ago, told the story of how Earl Jellicoe, a British naval officer, was comforted by a letter from King George. "In the midst of a sea battle when Earl Jellicoe was being misunderstood by the nation he served faithfully, a letter came from King George, whose keen sea sense had penetrated the mist which had bemused the general public. His letter heartened the fleet. What did anything matter now? Their king knew."

"Sometimes," Amy Carmichael commented, "circumstances are so that we must be misunderstood, we cannot defend ourselves, we lie open to blame, and yet we may know ourselves clear before God—and man—in that particular matter."[2]

The King of our lives knows! If we are to blame, it cannot be hidden from Him. And when we are unjustly criticized or condemned, He understands. In either case, He wants to join with us in a majority opinion of two that, no matter what has happened, we have a bright future and can press on without dreading the next rejection.

THE HEALING POWER

That's not all. Christ is the healing power of the world. And just as He can heal our bodies, He can miraculously heal our broken hearts. When we surrender our hurts to Him, He mysteriously works within our thoughts and feelings to set us free.

When rejections come, our first response should be to confess that we can't "take" them alone. When I'm hit with a rejection, I often think of Elisha A. Hoffman's hymn:

> I must tell Jesus all of my trials;
> I cannot bear these burdens alone;
> In my distress He kindly will help me;
> He ever loves and cares for His own.

Sometimes the healing comes quickly. More often it takes place over a period of time. Like a compound fracture or a concussion, a broken heart takes time to heal.

In the healing process, we begin to refocus our self-image and see ourselves as people loved and accepted by the Lord. That realization gives us the courage to embrace ourselves. Even though we have made mistakes that caused people to reject us, the Lord forgives us and gives us the power to forgive ourselves.

At the same time, if the hurt has been caused by distorted attitudes in those who have rejected us, Christ gives us the strength to forgive them. He reminds us of all the people we've hurt by rejection. That usually makes us much more ready to understand and let go of our anger.

PLEASING THE WRONG PERSON

At this point in the healing process, the Lord reminds us that our hypersensitivity to people's attitudes may be caused by trying to please the wrong people. We will not be free from the potential hurts of rejection until we make pleasing God our first priority. What God thinks of us is the only thing that's ultimately important. And He has already expressed His pleasure in us by choosing and calling us to be His disciples and intimate friends.

The good news is that God's pleasure in us does not vacillate with our performance. When we fail, His love for us is steady and sure. His forgiveness is offered before we ask. And when we are rejected because we've been faithful to Him in living out our faith, He strengthens our courage to stick by our convictions.

Our goal as disciples is not to win a popularity contest but to serve the Master. Obedience to Him often runs counter to the values of our culture. We *will* get into trouble because of what we believe. Our stand on social issues may bring criticism and hostility, and our priorities will make us targets for ridicule.

I'm convinced that the reason so few of us Christians share our faith with others is that we fear rejection. Think of the times we haven't talked about what Christ means to us because we feared being categorized as pious prudes. Or recall those times when we remained silent while a person's character was assassinated with gossip, or ideas were expressed that were contrary to our convictions.

Our reluctance to do battle for truth reminds us that we're playing our lives for the wrong audience. Of course, there's a constructive way to stand for what we believe: grappling with issues rather than expressing our views with argumentative arrogance.

The other day I overheard and observed a friend communicate his convictions in a very winsome way in a conversation with a group of men. For every negative comment made, he had a positive thought to add. When people were put down, he balanced the maligning criticism with affirmation. And when problems of contemporary life were discussed, he gave a clear witness to how Christ had given him power to face and solve his own difficulties. The group couldn't "write him off" because of the authentic way he shared what he believed. Interestingly enough, he's the person many of these men turn to when they face problems.

Our Lord calls us to greatness. That greatness involves strong convictions we cannot compromise and actions we must take because of our faith. When we have decided to please the right person, Christ, for the right reason and in the right way, rejection may be a sign that we are making an impact. But the blows of rejection are softened by the deflecting shield of His pleasure. And we needn't live in fear of the rejection, protected by His strong shield.

LOOKING OUTWARD

As we allow Christ to heal the hurts of rejection and release us from the fear of its recurrence, we can become amazingly free to turn our attention away from ourselves to others, who are suffering from rejection—and fear of rejection—themselves. As "wounded healers" we are equipped to care and console.

As we turn our attention away from our own pain, we may see that the "hits" we take from people are often rooted in frustrations they are going through that may have nothing to do with us. As we become less sensitive to what they do and say, we can become much more sensitive to their needs.

Ruth Harms Calkin, in her book *Tell Me Again, Lord, I Forget,* relates her own experience of learning to care about someone she thought had rejected her. In a free verse poem entitled "Sensitize Me, Lord," she writes of taking offense that someone at a bus stop had not spoken to her. But minutes later the woman said, "Forgive me—I didn't see you." And then painfully described her personal crisis: a son diagnosed with leukemia. In reflection, Calkin asked God for forgiveness—for being so sensitive and taking offense when no offense was intended, for not seeing and immediately addressing the woman's need.[3]

There are people all around us who are suffering inside, those who look so very polished on the surface. Remember, those who reject us are probably aching over some pain, or maybe rejection, in their own lives. Christ wants to give us the security in Him that frees us to minister to the needs of others rather than worrying constantly about our own.

THE FINAL STAGE OF HEALING

The final stage in Christ's healing comes when we praise Him for all of the times He's used people to affirm and encourage us. The psalmist found great relief in remembering God's goodness.

> I would have lost heart, unless I had believed
> That I would see the goodness of the Lord
> In the land of the living.
>
> PSALM 27:13

Reflection on the faithfulness of God produced the psalmist's positive expectation of seeing further evidences of His intervening grace.

In a real way, we get what we look for. As I said earlier, if we expect rejection, we'll probably signal our fear to others. It may be this fearful attitude they reject as much as anything. We all abhor our own hypersensitivity to being rejected so much that we intensely dislike it in others.

Remember Allison, who discerned that she had sometimes "received what I ... feared"? Here's how she finishes her story:

Now I am discovering a new way of life. I've been a Christian for a long time ... but I've been a Christian focusing on myself and my fears. Now I am finding that total abandonment to Jesus, and focusing on Him, is my hope. He has begun a healing process in me. I now can see people who have hurt me as the hurting people they are. This helps me experience not only receiving God's grace and mercy but also sharing it.

I am learning to move away from my fear and expectations of rejection as I turn to Jesus for His acceptance and approval. And now I'm amazed at the way He loves me through people I had previously expected to reject me.

BECOMING AN ENCOURAGER

As I look back over the years, I see how the Lord has strategically placed people in my life who believed in me and spurred me on.

I've come to believe that the Lord balances the scales: When someone rejects us, He sends someone else to encourage us. In fact, when I am downhearted, I actually eagerly anticipate the person God will use to mediate His uplifting love. I pray, *Well, Lord, who will it be this time?* I've never been disappointed. I've seen the goodness of the Lord in the unexpected encouragers who have communicated hope.

I think such people are there for all of us—if we open our eyes and *look* for them. Having had the help of encouragers through the years, I long to be an encourager to others. And I never lack for opportunities. People express their needs by their tone of voice, the expression on their faces, and in their body language. Life is difficult for most people. A ministry of encouragement leaves us little time to nurse our own feelings of rejection.

In my Senate Bible studies, we've discussed the people in our lives who have made the greatest impact on us; we considered what we remembered most about them. The majority of us talked about those who had encouraged us and through that affirmation had earned the right to share their faith with us. A large number of us had been introduced to Christ by an encourager whom Christ had put in our lives. The discussion pushed us to ask ourselves, "How many of us are encouragers?"

The Lord delights in surprising us in the way He sends people to us when we need help and in the opportunities He gives us to help others. That makes life an exhilarating adventure.

WAIT ON THE LORD

Knowing that the Lord is at work gives us the patience to wait for Him to act. Psalm 27 concludes with that seasoned wisdom:

> Wait on the Lord;
> Be of good courage,
> And He shall strengthen your heart;
> Wait, I say, on the Lord.
>
> VERSE 14

We do not have to wait for the Lord to come to us, for He has never left us. What we must wait for is the complete fullness of His healing. Is there a way to speed up the healing process? Yes, by trusting Him with our hurts sooner rather than later. I say that because the Hebrew word translated *wait* actually means "trust in confident expectation."

Few things make us more aware of our need for the Lord than rejection. The only final cure for the frowning face of rejection is His smiling face of love and acceptance. And the more we wait for Him, the less we'll wait in fear of future rejection. I say it again:

> Wait on the Lord;
> Be of good courage,
> And He shall strengthen your heart.

Chapter Eight

WHO'S IN CONTROL HERE?

PRESCRIPTION 8:

*Turn over control of your life to the Lord. Trust His
control over what you were never meant to control.
Take responsibility for what He has given you to do
for His glory and by His power.*

Years ago, when my son Andrew was riding with me in the car, he
noticed my bad habit of putting my left foot on the brake and my
right foot on the accelerator.

"Dad," he said, "you can't put on the brakes and go forward at the same
time!"

We both laughed, but it made me think about people I know who fear
losing control. They have a heavy foot on the brakes of their lives all the
time!

When I asked people in my national television audience to write me
about their greatest fears, one woman wrote a very frank letter.

"You asked us to be honest about our fears. So instead of giving you
some trite, quick answer, I really thought about it. And the more I did, the
more I realized that the most frightening thing for me would be to lose
control.

"Oh, I don't mean flying off the handle. More than that, it's the fear of not always being able to determine what happens to me. Over the years I've liked being boss over things. I feel very insecure when I can't manage things—my home, my family, situations. That may be wrong but that's the way I am!"

I appreciated the woman's honesty. To a lesser or greater degree, all of us need to be in control.

It starts when we realize the awesome responsibility we have for our own lives. Early in life we discover that there's a direct cause-and-effect correlation between our choices and what happens to us. What we do and say brings both good and bad results. The pain of failure makes us want to avoid further hurt. We vow to work harder to assure success.

That's when we slam on the brakes. Avoiding failure becomes an obsession. Our grip on life becomes tighter. The thought of losing control makes us panic. We keep life's challenges pared down to what we can handle without failure. Having been hurt, we control how vulnerable we will become. Much of life is held at bay.

The process doesn't stop there. Even if we do nothing, we can be injured by other people's mistakes. The only way to prevent that is to control their lives, too. By telling our families, friends, and neighbors where to go, when, and at what speed, we hope to ensure the safety of our own vehicle. Besides, pushing people around gives us a feeling of power and competence. It soothes our secret feelings of failure.

Sometimes our techniques of domination are quite obvious: "Do what I want or else!" we threaten. But a pout can be just as effective as a shout when we don't get our way. Affirmation and affection are often withheld until people get back on the track doing what we want.

People aren't helpless puppets, though; they fight back. "Why do you always have to do it your way?" they ask. "Who's in charge here?" Power struggles develop in marriage, in family life, in friendships at work, in the church, and in the community.

A recurring theme of my discussions with senators on how to receive supernatural power for leadership is the necessity of surrendering control of their lives and careers to the Lord. Some of the most crucial reaffirmations of faith between both senators and key staff have revolved around this liberating release from the tenacious grip on life, relationships, and the future. Sometimes it is not easy for the Holy Spirit to peel back the icy fingers of a leader's need to control everything to assure success or to stay in office.

One man described his experience in a Bible study prayer time. He said he felt the control rush out of him almost like losing his breath. Then in a desperate gasp he invited the living Christ to take up residence within him and take control.

The fear of losing control weakens the most important relationship of life ... our relationship with Christ. It keeps us from experiencing the full joy and delight of the abundant life.

Christ loves us and offers us His power. All He asks is that we accept His absolute control. He expects us to surrender our wills to do His will and commit our total lives—all that we are and have—to Him. Then He promises us His wisdom for our decisions, His supernatural strength for our challenges, and His love for our relationships. That's not a bad offer!

LIFE'S BIGGEST STRUGGLE

And yet our need to be in charge of ourselves, others, and situations often makes our relationship with Christ life's biggest power struggle. We are reluctant to relinquish our control and allow Him to run our lives. We may believe in Him and be active in church and good causes, but trusting Him as Lord of everything in life can be scary. Even though we pray about our challenges and problems, all too often what we really want is strength to accomplish what we've already decided is best for others and ourselves.

Meanwhile we press on with our own priorities and plans. We remain the scriptwriter, casting director, choreographer, and producer of the drama of our own lives, in which we are also the star performer.

Over the years I've discovered that life really begins with a total commitment to Jesus Christ. I've also discovered that this decision is the missing dynamic in most Christians today. Many began the Christian life with a belief in Christ as Savior. But the implications of accepting Him as Lord of all life were either not made clear or, if they were, not taken seriously.

I was a Christian for eight years before I actually committed my life to Christ. Up to that point, I struggled constantly to stay in charge and get Christ to help me do what I thought was best. The joy and freedom I felt when I finally handed my life over to His control made discipleship an exhilarating adventure.

And yet I've found that I have to renew that commitment every day. As a strong-willed person, I often forge ahead with my own plans and strategies. When I make a mess of things, I realize that I have taken charge again and need to resign the management of life to Christ all over again. As I do, the floodgate is opened to the flow of His guidance for my decisions. I find His answers for my perplexities, His solutions for my problems, and His love and patience for the people around me. Once again, He intervenes to meet my challenges in unexpected and delightful ways.

I'm thankful to have discovered the secret of commitment early in my ministry. Through the years it has made me aware of my need to surrender control. It has also helped me to identify the fear of losing control in other people. I've enjoyed helping uptight, tied-down people experience the freedom of allowing Christ to run their lives.

The highly controlled person finds it difficult to trust Christ profoundly. Living by faith—the daring, adventuresome faith that can meet tough challenges—is risky. Feeling threatened, we shrink back and refuse to take responsibility for what the Lord has put in our charge.

That leads us to the next powerful prescription for fearless living: *Turn over control of your life to the Lord. Trust His control over what you were never meant to control. Take responsibility for what He has given you to do for His glory and by His power.*

A PARABLE ABOUT IRRESPONSIBLE CONTROL

In the parable of the *minas* in Luke 19:11-27, Jesus introduces us to this important prescription. He reveals that the fear of losing control leads to failure in the very things He's assigned us to accomplish with trust in Him.

A nobleman was about to go into a far country to receive a kingdom. Before he left, he called ten of his servants to him. He gave each a *mina,* the equivalent of approximately one hundred days' wages for an average agricultural worker. "Do business until I return," the nobleman said, charging the servants to invest and multiply the minas.

When the nobleman returned, endowed with the kingdom and the right to reign over the realm, he demanded an accounting from his servants. Three made their reports. One had used his mina to earn ten. He was praised and handsomely rewarded. "Well done, good servant, because you were faithful in a very little, have authority over ten cities" (v. 17). The second had earned five minas with his investment. Though he did not receive the same commendation as the first, he was rewarded with equal measure for his productivity and placed in control over five cities.

The third servant, however, reported, "Here is your mina, which I have kept put away in a handkerchief. For I feared you, because you are an austere man. You collect what you did not deposit, and reap what you did not sow" (vv. 20-21). Out of fear rooted in totally false assumptions about the nobleman, the servant had hidden away the mina and had no profit to show.

A dramatic twist occurs at the end of the parable. Dismayed by the servant's cautious unproductivity, the nobleman took his one mina away and gave it to the servant who had multiplied his investment to ten minas. I think the main part of the parable ends at this point.

In verse 25, however, there is a parenthetical remark that at first seems to be part of the parable. "But they said to him, 'Master, he has ten minas.'" I suggest that this remark is by Jesus' disciples, who interrupted him because of the sudden, astounding turn in the parable when the unprofitable servant's one mina was given to the one who had ten. The disciples were following the story with keen, rapt attention and blurted out their astonishment at what had happened to the one-mina man.

We can understand the disciples' strong reaction. Jesus has our attention also. One of His most disturbing statements follows with a laser thrust. It's really a warning to those who fear losing control. "For I say to you, that to everyone who has, more will be given; and from him who does not have, even what he has will be taken away from him" (v. 26).

The Lord has turned the table of our values upside-down! What does this mean? "To everyone who *has* ..." Has what? What does that mean for us? To answer that, we need to go back over the parable and reflect on its implications for us.

Right from the beginning of Jesus' parable, we catch the autobiographical tone. Clearly, Jesus is the nobleman of the parable. After the cross and resurrection, He would ascend to heaven, receive the Kingdom from His Father, and return as reigning Lord. Remember that His kingdom means His rule over those of us who are called to belong to Him as faithful and obedient disciples. We enter that kingdom by the gift of faith He gives us, and we live in its full joy as we accept the responsibility He gives us.

The rest of the parable is really our story. Each of us is one of the servants. Which one of the servants best represents how you've used the mina entrusted to you?

A CLOSER LOOK AT THE SERVANTS

All three servants had two things in common. All were given one mina, and all were given the same opportunity to invest and multiply it. What does the mina represent for us?

I believe that the mina is *the gift of faith*. All of us receive the basic gift of faith. It is not earned or deserved. It is freely given to us to respond to the love, forgiveness, and reconciliation of the cross.

By faith we are given the power to believe and accept Christ as Lord and Savior and turn our lives over to His control. That's the beginning of the adventure of the abundant life and the assurance of eternal life.

The same gift of faith that reconciles us to the Lord also releases us to follow His orders in every area of daily life. He gives us—all of us—a new life to live for His glory. But it's in our response to that gift that the similarity between Christians often ends.

Just as the three servants in Jesus' parable had two things in common, there were two radical ways they differed. There was a difference in what they did with their minas and how they were rewarded.

What does that mean for our mina, our gift of faith? The most obvious answer is that faith is given to us to help us grow in our relationship with the Lord. Trusting His control of our lives produces growth in intimacy with Him and in the transformation of our character and personality in His image. We invest our mina as we pray in the words of the old hymn by Adelaide Pollard:

> Have Thine own way, Lord ...
> Mold me and make me after Thy will...
> Hold o'er my being absolute sway.

Multiplying our mina of faith means bringing all facets of our life under God's control. That includes marriages, families, friendships, work. Christ is Lord of all. His lordship extends to every realm as we surrender to Him what we do, say, and seek to be His person.

Now we are ready to look at the second thing that the servants in Jesus' parable did not have in common. They were rewarded differently for their use of their mina. Two were rewarded to the extent that they multiplied what had been given to them. The one who hoarded his mina had it taken away. The servant's refusal to multiply his mina also underlines a basic truth of life: *We lose what we do not use.*

Why did the man hoard his mina? I propose that he was afraid of losing control. When confronted with his lack of return, the servant tried to cover up his fear by questioning the nobleman's character. His accusation that the nobleman was austere, collecting what he had not deposited and reaping what he had not sown, could not have been further from the truth.

The cautious servant refused to take responsibility for investing and multiplying the nobleman's mina. I think he feared doing something wrong and ended up doing nothing at all. Behind his pretentious exterior of superior prudence was a highly developed habit of control. The one-mina man was determined to run his own life. He ventured nothing and he got nothing. He lost what he had. This servant who refused to serve is the "patron sinner" of controlling people in every age.

WHAT DOES THIS MEAN TO US?

We must ask, what does this mean to us? Clearly, the fear of failure is beneath the surface of our desire to be in control. The memory of previous failures keeps us from taking risks. We accept our mina of faith and keep it within safe, controllable boundaries. When life makes its demands and inflicts its problems, we are too scared to venture beyond what we are sure we can handle. A vague belief in Christ provides little help. As a result, we feel alone, defenseless, and filled with anxiety.

Then, like the cautious servant, many of us try to shift the blame. We complain about the Lord's management of things. We are quick to question why He has allowed us to have difficulties. The gift of faith goes unused and untested in receiving the Lord's power for the very questions and difficulties we face. Like the fearful servant in the parable, we seldom use the mina of faith, and therefore it never really becomes ours.

We should not be surprised that the nobleman took the mina from the cautious servant and gave it to the servant who had ten. Why should he care? He neither claimed his mina nor used it for the purpose for which it was given to him. So, too, those of us who have been given the gift of faith to believe in Christ fail to appropriate the gift when we insist on maintaining absolute control of our lives. Opportunities to invest our faith come and go without our trusting the Lord for His strategy and strength.

That explains the application of Jesus' words, "For I say to you, that to everyone who has, more will be given; and from him who does not have, even what he has will be taken away from him" (Lk 19:26).

An untested, uninvested faith is no faith at all. Many of those who join the church say yes to carefully worded questions about their belief in Christ but then go on living self-dominated lives. When problems and challenges hit, they endure them as before, under their own control.

Should that faith be taken from them? That's really not necessary, because it was never genuine faith at all. Some churches may accommodate saying the right words without accepting Christ's authority and our responsibility, but Christ doesn't make that accommodation. He was absolutely clear about that in the Sermon on the Mount. "Not everyone who says to Me, 'Lord, Lord,' shall enter the kingdom of heaven, but he who does the will of My Father in heaven" (Mt 7:21). Accepting our responsibility to seek and do the Father's will requires complete trust in His Son who is with us to show us the way and provide the power to follow.

HUMILITY

Complete trust requires something else—humility. The fear of losing control is really pride. And pride is simply the refusal to be loved and to love. True humility is the opposite. A humble person is not a mealy mouthed, groveling bundle of self-effacement but a person who knows he or she is loved and gifted by God. Secure in that love, such an individual constantly points away from self to the source of strength. There's no room for the thought that he has all the answers for himself and others. Humility leads us to a right estimate of ourselves. And that estimate includes the realization that we are not omniscient, that we don't know everything and we never will.

Just telling people who are afraid of losing control that they should stop being afraid won't work. They—we—need to face the deep inner cause: pride that's masquerading as a "know-it-all" sufficiency.

The fear we feel is the product of a confrontation between the Lord's Spirit and our own spirit of pride. "God resists the proud, / But gives grace to the humble" (Jas 4:6). That resistance is registered in our souls first as fear. The Lord is invading our fortress of arrogance. Our defensive response is the fear of letting go. It is a sure sign that the Lord has singled us out for the breaking of our control over ourselves and others. The refusal to humble ourselves before Him sometimes means that He must humble us.

But the Lord never humiliates us. He has a much more effective way than that. He simply allows us to go on thinking we're running things until our control breaks down, and we see how ineffective it really is. Fearing failure, we are hit by even greater failures. The people we've tried to control rebel and let us know that they are tired of being held in our grip. Then life falls apart in some situation we've been ruling with an iron hand. At such times, the Lord goes right on loving us and will help us, if we ask Him, to recover from our foolish assumptions of self-sufficiency.

THE STORY OF MICHAEL

Michael was a good example of this. He was a strong-willed person. Just ask his family or the people who worked with him. He was a drill sergeant, an answer man, and an authority on almost everything—all rolled into one. Behind his forced smile was a tightly held jaw of determination. He was a take-charge person.

At home, things had to go Michael's way. At work, his constantly repeated "It's not in the budget!" squashed the creativity of others, but there was always money for what he wanted to do.

As an officer of his church, he enjoyed the recognition of his authority when pastors would say, "Better check it out with Michael. Nothing happens without his OK!"

The community organizations in his small town were always short of volunteers for leadership and Michael was more than ready to step in.

Yes, Michael believed in Christ. And yes, he prayed for the Lord to bless his busy life. But Michael was a proud man.

Some frightening failures had hit him early in his adult life. He determined never to let that happen again. He clamped down on himself and those around him to make sure everything was kept in control. Never having had a profound experience of the Lord's love, he developed defensive pride. Perfectionism covered his fear of failure. Humble was the last word people would have used to describe this religious man.

I met Michael at a retreat for men. His carefully controlled world had fallen apart. His daughter had rebelled in a way that exposed his failure as a father. A new pastor in his church had confronted him with the harm done by his imperious ways. On top of that, the members of his congregation had voted him out of his key position as a lay leader.

When Michael turned to his job to build up his ego, he found that some of his employees had reported to the president of the company how unhappy they were.

Michael's control was collapsing.

It seemed as though the whole retreat, which was about the joy of living under the control of the lordship of Christ, had been planned just for Michael. The Lord was closing in on him. And the miracle of the Lord's grace happened through the messages of the retreat leaders and the personal testimonies given by some of the other men. After several sleepless nights, wrestling with what he had heard, Michael saw his fear of losing control for what it really was—pride and fear of failure.

Near the end of the retreat, Michael and I had a long conversation. He poured out what was happening to him. After sharing my own struggle with giving the Lord control of my life, I told him about several people I knew who had overcome their tight control on life by surrendering their lives to Christ. We talked about his need to accept how much the Lord loved him and about the freedom that living under the Lord's control brings.

Because the Lord's Spirit was working in him, Michael was able to see what his lack of humility and his need to be in control had produced. Taking charge had kept him from his real responsibility of loving and helping the people around him. At the end of our time together, he confessed his pride, his fear of losing control, and his controlling ways in relationships. And he prayed an honest prayer of commitment to Christ.

Later in the day, Michael shared his commitment with the men in his small group, all of whom had come from his town. It was not easy to be open and honest about what he had gone through. Some of the men in the group had experienced Michael's self-assured, controlling personality firsthand and had decided that he would probably always be that way. They were amazed at what he told them. And the same Lord who had broken open Michael's heart was there to help the men be receptive and understanding. In fact, some of them were able to confess their own need for release. The group talked about how they could help each other in the future when the old pattern of fear reared its ugly head.

I'm happy to say that group of men has continued to meet. They have breakfast together every other week to talk about how to live under the management of the Master. When they see each other around the community, they greet one another with five uplifted fingers—a finger for each of the five vital words of their group's motto: "Relax, Christ Is in Control!"

Michael and his friends would be the first to tell us that the commitment they made at that retreat was only the beginning. The repatterning of their need to be in control continues daily. And the fear of losing control in some relationship or challenge is a warning signal that they have slipped back into old habits that don't work. The more they admit the tendency, the less it happens.

SIX WAYS TO ACCEPT CHRIST'S CONTROL

Each of us is different, and we all have our own ways of bucking the Lord's authority. What can we do about our fear of losing control? Here are six ways to accept Christ's control that summarize what I've tried to say in this chapter.

1. Admit that the need to be in charge of your life has resulted in a fear of losing control. Acknowledge that this is rooted in pride and that you need to receive more of the Lord's grace in your life.

2. Humbly tell the Lord about your panic over losing control. Accept His healing love and forgiveness for the limits you've placed on yourself and other people by always wanting to be in charge. Tell Him exactly what has happened under your insufficient management.

3. Make today the first day of a new beginning. Commit your life to the Lord's authority.

4. Experiment with trust and experience the results. Move quickly to the problems and needs you face right now. Take them one by one. Give them over to Christ's control.

5. Keep a logbook in which you record what you have committed to Christ and what happens. Write a few paragraphs daily about the results of living under Christ's control. Discover how He works and note what is happening to heal your fears.

6. Ask the Lord to assign you challenges with people and situations needing His love and power. Trust Him! Through you, He will do things you never thought could happen. The Lord wants us to experience the difference. He knows that we will not give up anxiety about not being in charge until we really feel the joy of living by faith in His control.

I firmly believe that anyone who follows these six suggestions for thirty days will experience an exhilarating release; you will never again be tempted to control everything and everybody.

Take your foot off the brake!

Chapter Nine

CAN YOU IMAGINE?

PRESCRIPTION 9:

Confess your fearful imagination and ask the Lord today, through His Spirit, to make your imagination a channel of His vision and not a breeding place for fear.

It happens when we least expect it.

Suddenly our peace of mind is invaded by frightening thoughts. Fearful possibilities flash on the screen of our minds as we picture in vivid detail the dire consequences of our actions.

Our concerns about the people we love are played out in tragic scenes. And the difficult people in our lives take leading roles as villains.

Fantasies are enacted on the stage of our minds, and we see ourselves saying and doing things that would be outrageous in real life. False pride makes us into heroes or heroines who achieve fame, wealth, and virtue in splendid scenes of pageantry.

All this takes place in the inner, hidden world of the imagination, one of the magnificent faculties of the thinking brain. Instead of using this marvelous, God-given ability in a positive way, we misapply it to exaggerate our most disturbing fears.

Any serious conquest of crippling fear in our lives must eventually confront the tendency of the imagination to produce illusory or unreal fears and to intensify our panic over those fears that do have some foundation in reality. An imaginary fear may be unreal, but a fearful imagination is very real.

Many people who responded to my survey of the causes of fear in their lives wrote simply, "imaginary fears." Some went on to explain that many of their worst fears never happened. And yet they continued to be victims of their gloomy imaginations.

REAL-LIFE EXAMPLES

For example, Brenda discovered a lump in her breast. Immediately she called a specialist for an appointment, but he couldn't see her for a week and a half. Brenda says those were the longest eleven days in her life. She was paralyzed by fear as she anticipated the worst possible diagnosis.

In her imagination, Brenda pictured a long illness and dramatized the excruciating experience of saying good-bye to her husband and children. She kept going over and over what it would be like to die of cancer.

When she finally did see the doctor and had some exploratory surgery, the lump turned out to be benign. But until she received that report, her imagination ran wild.

Or take Mark. He's constantly worried about his job. Each year he goes through agony in the weeks just before his annual review. He pictures his boss giving him a poor report or even putting him on notice.

That has not happened in the five previous yearly reviews, but Mark still imagines the worst. In reality, he's a conscientious worker and has every right to expect commendation. Instead, though, he anticipates criticism and imagines every negative detail of what might happen.

Vincent's situation is even more troublesome. Years ago his wife, Karen, had a brief infatuation with one of his friends. Fortunately, she saw very soon what was happening and put an end to it. But Vincent can't forget, and after all this time he still tortures himself with thoughts of the other men his wife might be attracted to. Nothing could be further from Karen's mind, but Vincent's irrational jealousy is eating away at their marriage.

Often our imaginations project negative pictures of our future.

Jack, a United Airlines captain, will be sixty years old in fourteen months. Until recently, he was looking forward to his retirement, but in the past few months inner feelings have alarmed him. Imagining life without the excitement of demanding flight schedules and the bustle of huge airports is bringing on periods of depression.

Finally, Jack talked to a psychologist. "What's happening to me? I'm frightened of being sixty. I dread retirement. Am I going crazy?" he wanted to know. His imagination was robbing him of the excitement and adventure God had ahead for him.

To a greater or lesser degree, we all face the problem of controlling the fear-producing power of our imaginations. As Ralph Waldo Emerson wrote:

> Some of your hurts you have cured
> And the sharpest you still have survived
> But what torment of grief you've endured
> From hurts that never arrived.

Unfortunately, enough hurts have arrived to intensify our fears about present problems. Bad memories tend to poison our imaginations. Past fears multiplied by present anxieties equal a fearful imagination. When we bring our hurtful memories of the past to the Lord for healing (Prescription 4), we lay the groundwork for this next liberating prescription for living without fear: *Confess your fearful imagination and ask the Lord today, through His Spirit, to make your imagination a channel of His vision and not a breeding place for fear.*

In applying this prescription, it is important that we understand what the Lord intended our imaginations to do and how we frustrate and distort His original purpose. Then we can claim His power to live out each day as fearless, imaginative, and healthy Christians.

IMAGINATION: TWO DISTORTED VIEWS

Before we examine how the transformation of our fear-filled imaginings can take place, we need to recognize and avoid two distorted views of the imagination that plague some Christians. I don't believe that either of these views can be supported by Scripture.

First, there are those who refuse to believe that the imagination is a God-given gift. People who hold this view have somehow twisted things around to where they see the imagination as unreal and sinful.

This idea finds its roots, in part at least, in a confusion that arose when the Hebrew Old Testament was first translated into the Greek version known as the Septuagint. In a number of places, the Hebrew word for *stubbornness* was translated into a Greek word that stood for the functions of the imagination.

Following that lead, the *King James Version* of the Bible uses the English word *imagination* to translate the Hebrew word for *stubbornness*. The *New King James Version* keeps the word *imagination* in most of the texts, but it clearly indicates in footnotes and margin notations that the word is *stubbornness* in the original Hebrew. The *Revised Standard Version* corrects the problem. For example, in the *King James Version* we read: "But they hearkened not, nor inclined their ear, but walked in the counsels and in the *imagination* of their evil heart, and went backward, and not forward" (Jer 7:24, italics mine). Notice the difference in the *Revised Standard Version:* "But they did not obey or incline their ear, but walked in their own counsels and the *stubbornness* of their evil hearts, and went backward and not forward" (italics mine). Other examples are found in Deuteronomy 29:19; Jeremiah 9:14; 11:8; 13:10; 16:12; and 23:17. From these examples you can see that if a person did not understand what had happened, it might be possible to equate the word *imagination* with evil and sinfulness.

The other distorted view of God's purpose for the imagination is called image-theology. People who cling to this simplistic idea believe that all they need to do is identify their needs and wants, then name them before God and claim the results.

Many who hold this point of view back it up by asserting that God is anxious to give us whatever we want. But that idea misses a crucial first step; we first need God's guidance in seeing what we should really need and want. The wisdom writer put it this way:

> Trust in the Lord with all your heart,
> And lean not on your own understanding;
> In all your ways acknowledge Him,
> And He shall direct your paths.
>
> PROVERBS 3:5-6

If we fail to ask God's guidance and simply imagine what we want and demand that God produce it, we are well on our way to indulging in self-centered pride and the presumption of putting ourselves in a position of authority over God.

The element that is missing in image-theology is seeking guidance from God about what we should ask for. Image-theology also fails to consider God's methods and timing. There's much more involved than the pagan notion that to have or be anything we want, we merely need to form a picture of it in our minds and then act as if it had already happened.

If we are to overcome both of these distorted views, we need to move on to examine God's gift of imagination. Putting it to its intended use will rule out our misapplying it and allowing it to become a seedbed for the germination and growth of our fears.

GOD'S GIFT OF IMAGINATION

Imagination is the God-given ability of the thinking brain to form and hold images of thought. It is the drama department of the mind, giving our ideas form and structure. It produces the motion picture version of our thought. With the imagination, we form the image of who we are; we envision what our lives can be; we work out solutions to our problems. Imagination is God's magnificent gift to us that opens the way to creativity, inventiveness, artistry, problem solving, and visionary leadership.

Most important of all, imagination gives us one of the most vital points for contact with the Lord's Spirit. It is a beachhead or entry point for the entry of His Spirit into our inner being. God gave us the ability to imagine so that He could implant His purpose and plan in our minds and help us discover His will for us.

Sadly, like our other abilities, our imaginations became flawed and distorted when sin entered the world through the disobedience of Adam and Eve. Imagination became a means for developing thoughts of rebellion and pride instead of being a channel for the Lord's vision and guidance. Our separation from God resulted in our thoughts becoming a target for Satan and the imagination becoming vulnerable to the influence of evil. God's own analysis of our plight was "the imagination of man's heart is evil from his youth" (Gn 8:21).

But God was faithful in His love and care for His fallen creation. He chose Israel to be His people through whom He would demonstrate His power and love. Then He called leaders and used their fallible imaginations to form the vision of His plan for His people.

The Old Testament biographies of these leaders are amazingly honest. They are accounts of human response and resistance, success and failure.

In these stories we see how patient God was in working with His people. In almost all of the heroes and heroines of ancient Israel, we find a startling mixture of use and misuse of the imagination in cooperating with God or in rebelling against Him.

Leaders like Abraham, Moses, Joshua, Gideon, Saul, David, Solomon, Elijah, and Jonah had vivid imaginations and clear vision. They accomplished great things when God was in control. But their stories also reveal the passionate struggle each had between God's vision and their human willfulness.

There were times when the imaginations of Israel's leaders were captured and enlivened by the Spirit of God, but their followers were dull and slow to respond because of the failure to catch the spark of God in their imaginations. The checkered history of their murmurings, rebellion, worship of other gods, and self-justifying legalism produced the most difficult periods in ancient Israel's history.

CHRIST AND IMAGINATION

The Good News found in our New Testament is that Jesus Christ, Author of life, through whom all things were made, came to redeem the functions of our minds and to transform us. Throughout His ministry He appealed to the imagination, honoring its function to form, hold, and achieve images.

By His use of moving parables, incisive metaphors, and stirring allegories, Christ chose to *show* His message of truth rather than simply tell it. He imprinted on people's imaginations the picture of what life was meant to be, the true meaning of His kingdom, and the joy of abundant and eternal life. His word pictures were so vivid that His followers were able to remember them years later and, under the guidance of the Spirit, preserve them in the Gospels.

But Christ did not come just to awaken His hearers' imaginations. He came to begin a new creation. His death and resurrection brought salvation to every part of human nature. Nothing was left out. And when we invite Him to live in us, the primary focus of His transforming work breaks the stranglehold of fear and liberates the imagination to become a servant of His Spirit in us.

A PROMISE FOR THE IMAGINATION

With Christ's death and resurrection and the outpouring of the Spirit at Pentecost, the promise given through Joel became a reality. "And it shall come to pass afterward," says God,

> That I will pour out My Spirit on all flesh;
> Your sons and daughters shall prophesy,
> Your old men shall dream dreams,
> Your young men shall see visions;
> And also on My menservants and on My maidservants
> I will pour out My Spirit in those days.
>
> JOEL 2:28-29

This is not only the prediction of the coming of the Spirit at Pentecost, but is also the promise of the renaissance of the imagination.

One of the most astounding contrasts of history is the change in the imaginations of Jesus' disciples after Pentecost and the infilling of Christ's Spirit. Prior to Jesus' death and resurrection and their being anointed with His Spirit, the disciples were fearful, vacillating, dull men who just couldn't understand what Christ was saying. After Pentecost, it all made sense to them, and what they were to be and do was unmistakably clear. With Christ-filled imaginations, they exemplified the new creation He had called them to experience and live. With the image of Christ as the focus of their imaginations, they grew in His likeness. Their fears were no longer exaggerated by their imaginations, but His promises were turned into specific hope for their own lives and what He would do through them.

Our imaginations are transformed when Christ anoints us with His Spirit. Our part in receiving His anointing is to confess the fears that dominate our imaginations and to ask for the panic-dispelling anointing of His Spirit. Just as His perfect love casts out fear of judgment, so too His indwelling Spirit captivates our thoughts and works to reshape them in our imaginations so we can picture His plan for our lives.

Christ wants to give us a new self-image—a vision of ourselves filled with His Spirit and completely under His control. Then He wants to help us to imagine what He can do for our problems and our relationships.

Turpentining the Imagination

What James Weldon Johnson prayed for the preacher in "Listen, Lord" should become our daily, moment-by-moment prayer for ourselves.

> Lord, turpentine his imagination,
> Fill him full of the dynamic of Thy power.

The anointing of the Spirit of Christ acts like turpentine on our varnished imaginations. Many of us who believe in Christ as Lord and Savior still have imaginations that are layered with the negative varnish of reserve and caution. Years of seeing reality only with our limited potential have encrusted our imaginations with memories of weakness and failure. As a result, the only things we can picture are repetitions of frightening things we've already endured.

When we ask the Lord to captivate our imaginations, He does what turpentine does to the layered varnish and paint on a piece of wood. He softens the hard layers, scraping them off until our imagination can be penetrated by His Spirit. Only then can we receive His guidance in vivid, dramatized images of His plans for us.

It's All in Your Imagination

We've heard those five words, "It's all in your imagination," all through our lives. That saying has been used more than once to convince us that our fears were hallucinations or self-deceptions, dismissing them as absurd or exaggerated.

Actually, the saying is accurate, but not in the ways it's customarily used. I want to say "It's all in your imagination" with a different meaning—stressing the importance of the imagination rather than ridiculing it.

All thought is processed by imagination. That's why a Christ-anointed imagination is so vital. Without that liberating gift our worst anxieties will be aggravated and intensified.

The circuit between our imaginations, emotions, and body systems will be activated. Powerful feelings of fear will pump adrenaline into our bloodstream. Inordinate stress will result. Many people live in that agitated state most of the time.

The only way to reverse the process is, indeed, all in our imaginations. And Christ can do it. When we surrender our imaginations to His control, He actually blocks some fears from entering. Others He reorients by showing us how He will be bringing the best out of troublesome situations. Most of all, He keeps our imaginations so busy picturing what He wants us to be and do that there's little time left to look for new things to worry about.

The Lord wants to set us free to focus on His strategy for our lives. We can't serve Him effectively if we are crippled with a fearful imagination. And yet, He waits for us to ask for the transforming miracle of His anointing.

MY PERSONAL EXPERIENCE

I can vividly remember the time, early in my ministry, when I first prayed for the anointing of Christ on my own imagination. A disturbing question had kept tumbling around in my mind. Why was I and why were most of the people I knew paralyzed by fear? We lived in two worlds: our outer world of challenges and opportunities and our inner world of hidden fears. Though we believed in Christ, there was little evidence of boldness or courage as we confronted our problems.

As individuals, we were worried and cautious. As participants in the church, we were fearfully bound to the securities of our sober doctrines and cherished traditions. Vision and vitality were lacking.

In my search for answers, I kept tripping over the biblical phrase "the fullness of God." Paul's prayer for the Ephesians alerted me to what I might be missing:

That Christ may dwell in your hearts through faith; that you, being rooted and grounded in love, may be able to comprehend with all the saints what is the width and length and depth and height—to know the love of Christ which passes knowledge; that you may be filled with all the fullness of God.

EPHESIANS 3:17-19

As I reflected on these words, I came to see how little of God's fullness I had really experienced. Intellectual acceptance had not carried over into a vibrant and alive vision for myself and the church.

So I asked myself, *If I have been created to receive all of the fullness, have I responded with all of my life?* I thought about the faculties the Lord had given me: intellect, memory, emotion, will. These I had rigorously tried to commit to the Lord. And yet something was missing that kept me from linking what I believed to the life that I was actually living. And fearfulness filled that void.

One day during my prayer and Bible study, a question came to mind: *What about my imagination?* I had to admit that I had never thought of including imagination in my commitment to the Lord. That realization moved me into a profound study of the imagination.

It was then that I came to some firm convictions about the power of imagination. We are all in the process of becoming the people we imagine ourselves to be. How I see myself in imagination will be the person I become. Imagination is the marshaling faculty of the mind that puts thought into action. It unifies a person's will, emotions, and physical energies toward the accomplishment of the picture the imagination forms.

I also began to realize how our imaginations affect other people. We can limit or liberate what they become by the image we hold of them in our minds. If we picture other people as if they don't count, that's what they will become for us. They will probably fulfill our expectations of them.

In taking this a step further, I saw the vital role of the imagination in the making of our plans and in the development of our expectations for the future. Our selves, our families, churches, companies, and community organizations are all radically affected by the vision we have for what they can become.

It was at this point that I saw that I was using my imagination to promote fear and not faith. I saw that I desperately needed Christ's healing of my imagination.

In response to my need, I made a deep commitment of my imagination to the Lord and prayed for the fullness of His Spirit to fill it, heal it, and use it to help me see myself, other people, and the church the way He does. It was one of the turning points of my life.

The results were amazing. A few weeks after praying that prayer, I was delighted to realize that many of my persistent fears had not come back to mind. And when new fears surfaced, I claimed the Lord's healing and transformation of them. I began to pray, "Lord, help me imagine people as You see them." And I found new power to affirm their potential.

THE GIFT OF FAITH REPLACES THE GRIP OF FEAR

Now, years later, as chaplain of the Senate, I've had a wonderful opportunity to share these discoveries about the power of faith-induced, hope-inspired imagination. Each day I teach Bible studies to groups of senators, senators' spouses, and Senate staff. It is exciting to see leaders live under the plumb line of God's righteousness and justice and receive His Spirit to help them exercise the supernatural powers of wisdom, discernment, and, most of all, vision.

Recently, in a Bible study on 1 Corinthians 12, my "Thursday group" examined the two levels of faith: the faith that saves, assuring our eternal life, and the faith that sustains, assuring us of abundant living. Careful study of the difference between the faith that accepts Jesus as Lord and the momentary faith that trusts Him with daily specifics led us into a fresh understanding of the "faith to faith" referred to in Romans 1:17.

One of the leaders identified this promise of the gift of advanced, practical faith to trust the Lord with particular problems, people, and tough situations to be the secret for peeling back the icy fingers of fear that often gripped his heart, keeping him from being a joyous disciple. Later that afternoon, he came to my office.

"I want this gift of faith!" he exclaimed. "I want to be able to envision what is God's best and have the fresh infusion of faith to claim it and trust God to accomplish it on His timing."

Together we prayed, "Lord, baptize our imaginations. Help us to picture Your boldest, most adventuresome vision for our lives and our nation."

Increasingly, I hear the petition in our prayer meetings here at the Capitol, "Lord, what do You want? Transform our imaginations so we dream Your dream. Paint the picture vividly in our thoughts and help us move forward with You to accomplish Your vision by Your power and provision."

The power of a Christ-motivated imagination has had a profound impact on my life and ministry in my parishes and now among the six thousand people I serve as chaplain: senators, their families and staffs, and all of the support teams that make the Senate run smoothly. It is so crucial for leaders and those who work with them to envision the next steps in the unfolding of the American dream. Along with many of the senators in the Bible study group, I'm discovering that the gift of faith replaces the grip of fear so we can boldly grasp the Lord's vision.

THE SECRET PLACE

Receiving the Lord's vision requires quiet time to meet the Lord and listen to Him. Like the psalmist, I retreat to a "secret place" for daily renewal. The Lord is waiting there for me—and you! The psalmist knew about that place.

He who dwells in *the secret place* of the Most High
Shall abide under the shadow of the Almighty.
I will say of the Lord, "He is my refuge and my fortress;
My God, in Him I will trust."

PSALM 91:1-2, italics mine

The Hebrew word for *secret place* really means "shelter," a place of protection and refuge. The same idea is expressed in Psalm 23: "You prepare a table before me in the presence of my enemies." In the psalmist's time, if you could reach the tent or dwelling of a friend and sit down at his table, you would not be attacked by your enemies as long as you remained in the protecting presence of your host. For us, that place of refuge is the heart of God.

Jesus said,

Let not your heart be troubled; you believe in God, believe also in Me. In My Father's house are many mansions; if it were not so, I would have told you. I go to prepare a place for you. And if I go and prepare a place for you, I will come again and receive you to Myself; that where I am, there you may be also.

JOHN 14:1-3

I believe more is involved in Jesus' words than preparation of a place in heaven for us after we die. Rather, I am convinced that He meant He was going to Calvary to prepare a place for us in the heart of God, a place of love, forgiveness, reconciliation, and healing. Surely, that's what is implied by His promise that He would come again and receive us to Himself, so that where He is we may be also.

And so we ask, where is He now? He is with us to lead us into the mansions, the resting places of the Father's house now—daily, hourly. That's our "secret place" to which we can retreat for the reformation of our imaginations. It's there that our fearful thoughts are changed into images of hope. It is there that our perception for what might happen is exchanged for the Lord's picture of what He has planned for us.

I could not live without these visits to the secret place of the Most High. There, repeatedly, I commit my imagination to become an agent of the Lord's thought for me and my needs. I spread out before the Lord the real and perceived fears that are hassling me. Then the Lord gives me the picture of the person He wants me to become in both character and personality. He shows me His image of what He wants me to do and say in my relationships. And I receive His vision of people to replace my inadequate expectations for them.

The apostle Paul gives us a vivid description of what can happen to the imagination in the secret place:

Eye has not seen, nor ear heard,
Nor have entered into the heart of man
The things which God has prepared for those who love Him.

1 CORINTHIANS 2:9

The apostle goes on to make this astounding statement. "But God has revealed them to us through His Spirit" (v. 10).

What follows in 1 Corinthians 2 is an exciting explanation of how the Spirit, who knows the deep things of God and the depths of our need for inspiration in our imaginations, actually guides our thoughts, "that we might know the things that have been freely given to us by God" (v. 12). A little further on Paul adds, "For 'who has known the mind of the Lord that he may instruct Him?' But we have the mind of Christ" (v. 16). That is awesome! The Greek word for *mind* used here means "intelligence." What Paul is actually saying here is that we are offered the divine intelligence of Christ as the source of images formed in our imaginations.

HOW IT WORKS

In another favorite passage from Paul, we discover how the creative use of imagination works in the secret place.

> The Lord is at hand. Be anxious for nothing, but in everything by prayer and supplication, with thanksgiving, let your requests be made known to God; and the peace of God, which surpasses all understanding, will guard your hearts and minds through Christ Jesus.
>
> PHILIPPIANS 4:5-7

Christ is not only coming back again, but He is present with us now. He takes us by the hand and leads us into the secret place. There our anxious thoughts and fears can be spread out before the Lord in prayer, supplication, and thanksgiving.

Prayer, in this context, means calling upon the Lord and claiming His presence and power. We approach the Lord by telling Him who He is to us. He is *Jehovah-Shammah* the Lord Ever-Present, *Jehovah-Rapha,* the Lord Our Healer; *Jehovah-Shalom,* the Lord Our Peace. All this we know in and through His Son, Christ our Lord, Emmanuel, God With Us. Christ is the heart of God meeting our frightened hearts with love.

In confident trust we can offer our prayers. We can tell the Lord our problems and perplexities. We do that with thanksgiving. As we thank Him for the things that have driven us to the secret place of prayer, we not only remember the Lord's goodness in the past but fully submit our present needs to Him. Thanksgiving is the ultimate and final act of submission; we are not completely free of our difficulties until we have thanked the Lord for them and for His wisdom in allowing them.

Our imaginations become open to the pictures of what He wants to do only after we pray, "Lord, thank You for these problems. I praise You that You have chosen me to become a channel for implementing the divine solutions You will help me imagine. I trust my imagination totally to You and will live out the vision You have given me."

Only then does peace replace panic. Paul says that peace actually guards our hearts and minds. Christ *is* our peace (see Eph 2:14). He stands as the sentinel of our imaginations, holding off any invasion of fear that might disturb our sure vision of what we have been guided to do. His peace-infusing presence also helps us each step of the way in making the vision a reality.

In Colossians 3:15 Paul speaks of peace ruling our hearts. The Greek word translated *rule* also means "umpire." God's peace, indwelling in Christ, calls the plays, showing what is right or wrong for us to do. He not only guards the entrance to our imaginations, but also rules out things we might think of doing that would further entrap us in fear.

My friend Paul Baskin has experienced that. He's an outstanding contemporary Christian songwriter. I was profoundly moved by hearing him sing his song "The Secret Place." The last verse summarizes what happens to the imagination in the secret place of intimate prayer.

> In the secret place
> I see Your beauty
> In the secret place
> My thoughts are healed
> For You are Lord, You are Lord
> I will not be ashamed
> I will not be afraid
> For in Your likeness I'm made in the secret place.[1]

FAITH AND IMAGINATION

It is there, deep in the secret place, that the gifts of imagination and faith work together to overcome our fears. Our responsibility is to seek to know the Lord's will. It is His responsibility to implant in our yielded imaginations the clear, impelling vision of what He wants to do for and through us. Then He gives us the gift of faith to trust Him.

As the author of Hebrews puts it, "Faith is the substance of things hoped for, the evidence of things not seen" (Heb 11:1). We realize in our mind's eye what we must pray for with confidence and assurance. Actually, growing in faith depends on ever-increasing, fresh inspiration from our imaginations.

Recently, on a trip to Georgia, I ran into an old friend. He has a speech habit that has earned him the name "Get-the-Picture Eddie." Eddie is a great talker. His monologues are laced with colorful southern colloquialisms, metaphors, and allegories. But his desire to be understood prompts him to punctuate his seemingly endless flow of words with "Get the picture?"

Though the Lord never tires us with endless words, He is urgently concerned that we "get the picture" of His plan for our lives and of His specific guidance for the fear-producing problems we face in daily living.

RECAP

Here are the vital elements of this ninth prescription for living without fear.

1. Thank the Lord for the gift of imagination. Praise Him that by His grace it is possible to picture your life filled with the Lord's love, joy, and peace.

2. Confess to Him the ways you may have misused the gift and developed a fearful imagination.

3. Claim the truth that He died on the cross for the redemption of all your faculties, including your imagination.

4. Specifically ask for the anointing of His Spirit on your imagination.

5. Spread out your fears before the Lord and ask Him to transform your fearful picture of what might happen into a vision of what He wills you to do in those very situations.

6. Visit the secret place of intimate communion with the Lord at the beginning and end of each day and repeatedly throughout the day. Each time a new fear attacks, go there immediately for His perspective, peace, and power.

Chapter Ten

DEATH, WHERE IS YOUR STING?

PRESCRIPTION 10:

*Face your eventual physical death and claim that you
are alive eternally. Then you can live abundantly
without panic for the rest of your time on earth.*

When Russell Weston burst into the Capitol on July 24, 1998, he tried to go around the metal detectors. As officer Jacob Chestnut, an eighteen-year veteran of the Capitol police, tried to stop him, Weston pulled out a revolver and shot him in the head. Then the gunman ran down the hall as tourists screamed, "He's got a gun." When Weston reached the back door of Rep. Tom DeLay's office suite, he burst in. Special agent John Gibson drew his gun. In an exchange of fire with Weston, Gibson was fatally wounded, but not before he shot Weston in the leg.

The entire Capitol was in a frenzy. Panic gripped everyone. The pall of death hung heavily for days as we expressed our grief, tried to comfort the slain officers' families, and had a memorial service in the Rotunda of the Capitol.

The Capitol flags were immediately put at half-staff on that Friday afternoon after the shooting. For many of the officers and Senate staff, the flag has remained at half-staff both in remembered grief and lingering fear of a recurrence of the tragedy. Our Capitol is the most open, accessible national building in the world. It's the people's building. We visit it in affirmation of our freedom and our heritage.

I can remember making rounds to all the officers' stations on that Sunday. The officers were visibly shaken. There was fear in their eyes and on-board alertness. A few days later, at 6:00 A.M. at shift-changing time at the Capitol Hill police station, I led a special prayer meeting. We talked about the unsettled feelings of the officers.

I exercise in the Capitol-police gym, and sometimes my conversations with officers return to that haunting week of mourning. Some put on their bullet-proof vests for the first time; others found that they relived that dreadful day over and over again. One said, "I never used to think much of death. Now there's seldom a day when I don't think about it."

TALK OF DEATH CAN BE FRIGHTENING

You may find that talking and thinking about death is threatening. Most of us don't like to think about dying, much less talk about it.

On her seventy-ninth birthday Bette Davis was interviewed on the "Today Show." She expressed curiosity about her mortality. "I'm really curious about how I will go and what will happen. But my friends don't like it when I talk about it. 'Don't talk about it,' they say. 'We *don't* want to hear about it.'"

Even writing our wills can be an unsettling experience. We are part of a society that abhors aging and is constantly in search of cosmetics, therapeutic vitamins, diets, and health kicks to keep us looking young.

At the same time there is a frenzy to expose the ills of even the most common things we eat or do that may threaten our health. Scientists are constantly informing us of the latest danger in our diets. And each new discovery about illness sends many of us into a hypochondriac's tailspin, worrying that we may have anthrax or the latest flu, or that we may be candidates for some new type of cancer. This panic is only a symptom of our greater fear of death.

We all want to live full and healthy physical lives as long as we can. "And why not?" you may protest.

We love living. The thought of physical suffering, in whatever grotesque form it may take, is abhorrent to us. And the possibility of an untimely accidental death is equally alarming. Most of us have made our plans for years ahead. Thinking about leaving loved ones, friends, and the things we've accumulated is not only unpleasant, it's excruciating. There's so much to do, see, and experience. Lurking beneath our gusto for living is the grief we harbor about dying.

Unfortunately, many Christians, who should have the greatest freedom from the fear of death, are often no more confident than anyone else. We want Christ to help us live the abundant life now, but we give far too little thought to our eternal life. And often, when we are hit with sickness ourselves or face it in our loved ones, we find that the extent of our faith is our hope that Christ will intervene to heal us so that we can live longer. We lust for a long life. Quantity of years becomes more important than the quality of our lives. Since we try to think about death as little as possible, our faith is not stretched to include the vibrant confidence that, whether we live or die, we belong to the Lord.

The fear of sickness and death still lurks beneath the surface of our minds. An illness or the death of a loved one or friend can force us to think about death, and then we submerge this disturbing subject again and race on in the fast lane of living.

FAST-FORWARD TO THE BEGINNING

In the mid-1980s I heard Amy Harwell, a brilliant, talented, successful young woman, give a vibrant testimony. This may be surprising, considering the fact that Amy had been diagnosed as having cancer with a grim prognosis for the future.[1]

After hearing her speak, I had a good visit with her. I wanted to know more specifically how Christ had helped Amy overcome her fear of sickness and death. She used a moving metaphor: "When I was given my final prognosis, it was as if someone had pushed the fast-forward button on my videotape machine. I couldn't help playing through the tape to the probable end of the scene. Often we speak of fast-forwarding a videotape to the end. For me, facing my death and knowing I am alive forever was like fast-forwarding to the beginning!

"I'm not afraid of death anymore. In fact, panic over sickness is gone. However long I live physically matters so much less now, and I'm really free to live now and forever."

A fast-forward to the beginning! That's exactly what I pray this chapter will be for you and me. I want to speed up the videotape of our lives in our minds to our own dying. And, like Amy, I'm convinced that the experience, when done in the full assurance of Christ's victory over death, will be a liberating release from the fear of sickness and dying. We'll discover that claiming death as a transition in living—a new beginning and not an end—will be the start of a wonderful freedom to live more fully now and for however long we have left on this earth.

FACING THE FEAR OF DEATH

Overcoming the fear of death, like all the other fears we've considered, takes place when we confront it and take a bold step for living without fear. Here's my tenth "fearless" prescription: *Face your eventual physical death and claim that you are alive eternally. Then you can live abundantly without panic for the rest of your time on earth.*

The promise of Scripture I want to claim for this very crucial step honestly recognizes what the fear of death does to us and states what Christ has done about this life-sapping anguish. In 1 Corinthians 15:25-26, Paul says that we can be free from the first fear of the last enemy. "For He

[Christ] must reign till He has put all enemies under His feet. The last enemy that will be destroyed is death."

This verse boldly affirms Christ's reigning, triumphant victory over death. It also realistically recognizes that fear of death is still a formidable enemy for us. In the interval between Christ's resurrection and His return, physical illness and death will confront us. But through the miracle of our own personal, spiritual resurrection now and our regeneration into new people in Christ, we can know with assurance that our physical dying will be only a transition in the onward flow of our eternal life. Let's talk about how that happens.

CHRIST'S VICTORY

Conquest of the fear of death begins with Christ's death and resurrection. That's not just "Easter talk." It is the central fact that sparks faith and provides the solid reason for assurance. The preexistent Christ, the One through whom all things were made, the Author of life, the creating Power of God, lived among us as Life in all its fullness. He who said, "I have come that they may have life, and that they may have it more abundantly" (Jn 10:10), and "I am the way, the truth, and the life" (Jn 14:6), is the same Lord who suffered on the cross for our forgiveness and rose from the dead as victor over the power of death.

As the author of Hebrews summarizes so movingly, "Inasmuch then as the children have partaken of flesh and blood, He Himself likewise shared the same, that through death He might destroy him who had the power of death, that is, the devil, and release those who through fear of death were all their lifetime subject to bondage" (Heb 2:14-15).

That raises a question. The writer of Hebrews speaks of Christ's victory as finished. But remember, Paul said that Christ must reign until He has put all enemies under His feet, and that the last enemy to be destroyed will be death. Does that mean that Christ's victory over death is incomplete?

Not at all. Christ reigns as Lord to love us, to give us the gift of faith in Him, and to enable us to claim His triumphant defeat of death by rising from the dead. His resurrection is our personal assurance that death holds no power over us. It's more than an idea we accept; it's an experience that can transform us.

For that, we need a firsthand experience of the presence of the resurrected, living Lord and a personal realization that, because He lives, we also shall live now and forever. No secondhand experience of the Easter miracle will give us freedom from the fear of death.

A SECONDHAND EASTER?

There's a secondhand store in Hollywood, California, that touts the resale of wardrobes of the stars. For a price, you can buy, wear, and pretend you have the charisma of your favorite star of stage and screen. At least, that's the sizzle of the store's advertising.

During Holy Week, I drove by the shop and was amazed by a sign in the window. In bold letters it read, "Have a firsthand Easter with a second-hand Easter bonnet worn by a star!" I could hardly believe my eyes. Someone had spent a lot of time on the wording of that eye-catching sign!

You can imagine the seed of thought that sign planted in the furrows of my mind. It takes more than a secondhand hat worn by a celebrity, or even a new one, to have a firsthand Easter. The sign started me thinking about the kind of Easter that would be "firsthand" all year long. It is one in which we meet the risen Lord personally.

Actually, a secondhand experience will not be sufficient for our firsthand encounter with the fear of sickness and death. Rumored hope, hearsay faith from others, and inherited tradition won't help us when we come to grips with our physical limitations and mortality.

A good way to test how much of a firsthand experience we have had with the risen Lord and the power of His resurrection is to think and feel through how we would react if we were told that we had only one month left to live.

Would our relationship with Christ give us the courage we would need? Would His victory over death be our assurance that, in spite of our physical death, we are alive forever? This fast-forwarding of the videotape of our lives to our death not only shows us our real attitude about our own death; it also reveals a lot about the level of our intimacy with Christ.

I asked a group of five hundred people at a retreat, most of them church members, to write on a card how they would feel if they were told they had a short time left to live.

Seventy-five said they were ready and felt that they were sure of their relationship with Christ and eternal life through Him.

Two hundred twenty said, in a variety of ways, that the question had shocked them with how superficial their relationship with Christ really was and that they were not prepared to die.

One hundred sixty said they would feel cheated because they had so much more they wanted to do. Forty expressed concern over those they would leave behind.

Eighty said they didn't know. The rest of the group expressed discomfort, anxiety, and even anger that I'd raised the question. Everything from, "I wished you hadn't asked!" to "It's none of your business!" was written by the people in this category.

The rest of the retreat was an intense time of encounter with Christ. His Spirit used the question to touch the raw nerve of our fear of death and our lack of assurance of eternal life. That assurance can come only as a result of a firsthand relationship with Him. I'm thankful that by the end of the retreat we had Easter and Pentecost all rolled into one on a Saturday afternoon in October!

PREPARATION FOR DEATH

Preparation for death begins now. And it's so much more than claiming Christ's victory over the grave. That's only the beginning. The living Lord's greatest miracle is our resurrection, not just at the time of our physical death, but now. Without that, we are unprepared to die and unable to live triumphantly without fear.

Christ said, "I am the resurrection and the life. He who believes in Me, though he may die, he shall live. And whoever lives and believes in Me shall never die. Do you believe this?" (Jn 11:25-26).

Well, do you believe it? Yes, we say, but often in a vague way that does little to overcome our own panic about death. It is true that we claim Christ's promise when a loved one dies or when we are seriously ill. But often we are doing little more than clutching for immortality and wishing that in some mysterious way our physical death won't be the end. But even with that, we loathe the eventuality of death.

Why?

A belief that we will live forever does little to overcome our fear of death because, if that is all we have, we are haunted with a deeper fear—where and how we will spend our forever. That's why repeated affirmation that death is not an ending really makes us more fearful. It's what might happen after death that makes dying so frightening. That's why, to many, the idea of immortality is meaningless. Life after death? Who wants to live forever?

Only those people for whom heaven has begun now want to live forever. For the Christian, eternal life is now, through the life, death, and resurrection of Jesus. His promise wasn't just to "live forever." Instead, He gave us abundant life here and now.

THE ROCK OF EXPERIENCE

There is no substitute for what John Henry Jowett, preacher and writer of prominence early in the twentieth century, called "the rock of experience." We know only what we have experienced. When we confront the enemy of death there is no greater weapon than our own personal fellowship with the risen Lord. As He did battle with Satan and peeled back the fingers of his stranglehold on humankind with the grip of fear of death, so, too, He seals us with a protective shield against Satan's influence over our thinking and feeling.

Satan's strategy is to try to influence us with the false idea that this life is all there is, that death is a horrible ending, and that we really cannot be sure of the joy of heaven. He tempts us with pride's silly idea that if we were to die, our loved ones could not make it without us, that our hard work would be lost, and that our little world would collapse. Satan tries to sentimentalize everything. We get teary about the things we'll never get to touch again, favorite places we won't enjoy again, and pleasurable happenings we won't delight in ever again.

But in fellowship with the Lord, we are set free to enjoy life to the fullest, knowing that everything matters because nothing ultimately matters except our relationship with Him. As a part of loving God, we are free to love more profoundly than ever before, without demanding that those whom we love be our reason for living. We can use things with great joy without being dominated by the idea that we are what we possess. Our work is no longer our god, the source of our meaning and purpose. That releases us to work harder and better without stress or burnout. We can live every day with all stops out, as if it were our last day on earth, because we know it's only one more day in forever.

HERE'S HOW IT WORKS

Here's how Christ's promise works. Christ permeates our lives with the power of His grace. In countless ways, He shows us that the life we are living is no life at all in comparison with abundant life in Him. He helps us admit that we are sinners, separated from God. Persistently and tenderly, Christ creates in us a profound sense of our emptiness and loneliness. Lovingly, He forces us to see what we are doing to hurt others and ourselves. He faces us with the disturbing truth that our arrogant efforts to run our own lives are failing. Not even our good works or achievements qualify us for status with God or assurance of eternal life.

It's usually some crisis that breaks our pride, some challenge that convinces us we don't have what it takes, or some opportunity that's beyond us, that forces us to admit our need for Christ. For some people the hunger for Christ is realized at a time of failure. For others it surfaces in response to the needs of people and the cultural plight of the world. For still others the need for Christ is realized in the witness of Christians who are attempting honestly to live out their faith each day. The Lord will use whatever is necessary to break through our defenses and open us up to the reality of His love for us.

It is then that we begin to experience the joy of losing our lives to become disciples of Jesus. As His followers, we submit ourselves to His leadership in every decision, because we want Him to become the absolute Lord of our lives.

The great, good news of all time is that when we respond, accepting Jesus as Savior and committing our lives to Him as Lord, we are resurrected out of an old life into a new life in Him. It's then that heaven begins. And with it comes the exciting process of regeneration.

REGENERATION

Regeneration is rebirth and reformation. The Lord we've confessed must now become the One whose indwelling power conforms us to His image. We have a personal experience of Pentecost.

The well-known nineteenth-century devotional writer F.B. Meyer wrote about the night it happened to him. He was walking in the Cumberland hills in solitude, with this prayer surging in his heart: "If there is one soul more than any other within the circle of these hills who needs the gift of Pentecost, it is I: I want the Spirit, but I do not know how to receive Him; and I am too weak to think, or feel, or pray intensely."

Dr. Meyer heard an inner voice say: "As you took forgiveness from the hand of the dying Christ, take the gift of the Spirit from the hand of the living Christ." To this Meyer responded, "Lord, as I breathe in this whiff of warm night air, so I breathe into every part of me Your blessed Spirit!" Recounting his experience, Dr. Meyer said, "I took, and took for the first time, and I have been taking ever since."

When we invite Christ to abide in us, He takes up residence in our total being. From within He shapes the new person we are destined to be. Intellect, imagination, emotions, and will come under His inspiring, re-patterning influence. We have new perspective, passion, and power. Christ gives us a new outgoing and loving personality, a new zest for living to the fullest, a new freedom to know and do His will.

Now that Christ-filled, unified, and healed person inside us is alive forever. Our physical bodies will age and grow weak. They will endure sickness and eventual termination. But the spiritual body—our mind, soul, and spirit—will live forever. As surely as Christ was raised from the tomb, so, too, our true self will be lifted out of our bodies to the next phase of heaven that began here on earth.

THE SURE CURE OF FEAR

The only sure way to overcome fear of death is to die! That's more than a clever play on words. When we surrender our lives to Christ, we die to ourselves. In the hymn "Hark, the Herald Angels Sing," Charles Wesley joyfully proclaimed this truth: Christ was

> Born that man no more may die,
> Born to raise the sons of earth,
> Born to give them second birth.

Those who have experienced the second birth need not fear the second death. Our first (spiritual) death happened when Christ was born in us. Our second (physical) death, whenever we leave our physical bodies behind, will be like going to sleep and awakening to our next day in heaven.

TO LIVE IS CHRIST

In a magnificent way, Paul fast-forwarded the videotape of his life when he wrote to the Philippian Christians during his imprisonment in Rome: "With all boldness, as always, so now also Christ will be magnified in my body, whether by life or by death. For to me, to live is Christ, and to die is gain" (Phil 1:20-21).

The apostle really believed that death would be a gain, a fuller union with Christ. I am convinced that we cannot say, "For me to live is Christ," until we have said, and meant, "for to die is gain." When we have thought through our dying, we are ready for abundant living. No longer do we have to cling to the days and years of our physical life on earth as if they were all there is.

Mysterious as it may seem, an anticipation of heaven gives us a greater excitement about living now. Knowing that we are going to live forever frees us to live now with greater gusto.

Alexander Maclaren, the great nineteenth-century Scottish preacher, said that this anticipation is the "true anesthetic which will give us a 'solemn scorn of ills' and make even the last and greatest change from life to death of little account."

It's fascinating to note that after Paul affirmed Christ was his life in dying or living, he could turn his attention more vibrantly to the needs of the Philippians. "Nevertheless to remain in the flesh is more needful for you. And being confident of this, I know that I shall remain and continue with you all for your progress and joy of faith, that your rejoicing for me may be more abundant in Jesus Christ by my coming to you again" (Phil 1:24-26).

Our Two Priorities

Paul's peace about dying renewed his passion for his two priorities—Christ and the needs of people. Christ was not only his Savior and Lord but also the very air he breathed, the pulse beat of his passion, the captivating thought of every moment. Christ was the indwelling power of Paul's mind, emotions, and will. Having died to himself when he surrendered his life to Christ, he became a postresurrection dwelling place of the Holy Spirit. A new man arose in his inner being who could no more be ended by physical death than the grave could hold the crucified Lord Jesus. It was this assurance that gave Paul a courageous assertiveness, a bold audacity. All of his passion for living became focused on his desire to care for the deepest needs in people—to meet and know Christ personally and experience the confidence of eternal life. To Paul, physical death was little more than a transition to the next and greater stage of life in Christ.

The people I know who have put fear of death behind them have this same passion for living. No longer having to cram life into the brief years that will be carved on their gravestone, they live each day to the fullest because they know they are alive forever. And the distinguishing quality of their lives is that they really care about people. Relationships are their top priority. There's no frantic rush about them. They have time to listen, care, and enjoy people. After all, what's the hurry when you know you're living one more day in forever?

GRACE FOR GRAY DAYS

There's no better tonic for life's gray days than that! So many days for most people are gray, not bright with blessings nor dark with bleakness, just gray with boredom. They endure the grayness in anticipation of some exciting event to brighten up the dullness, some new possession to capture their attention for a time, some thrilling trip to get away from it all. But this is not true for a person who can say, "To die is gain, for me to live is Christ." For this person, there's a relaxed purposefulness to all of life.

When John Wesley was asked what he would do if he knew that a particular day was his last, he responded with unfrenzied calm that he would read the Bible, pray his prayers, preach, and have tea with some friends: no different from most of his days. And yet, with that freedom from panic, Wesley traveled 225,000 miles, mostly on horseback, and preached 40,000 times until the day of his death.

Wesley's dying words were, "And best of all—Christ is with us." Then he went on to heaven for a continued realization of the fullness of Christ. But heaven had begun one day at Aldersgate when Wesley's heart was "strangely warmed" by the infilling of Christ's Spirit. After that, all of his hardships, conflicts, and difficulties were taken in stride. The days of the earthly portion of Wesley's eternal life were anything but gray. They were filled with the brightness of Christ's presence.

Are there Christians like that today? Yes! And you and I are meant to be among them. We can live without the fear of death. It's all a matter of believing in the risen Christ, knowing Him firsthand, experiencing the power of His resurrection and regeneration in us, and beginning the joy of heaven now.

AN AFFIRMATION OF FEARLESS CONFIDENCE

How can we be sure of a faith that wipes out all fear of death? I believe this happens as the following affirmations become a present reality in our lives:

I believe in Jesus Christ as my Savior. He died on the cross for my sins to set me free of guilt and condemnation. I know that I am loved and forgiven. Old memories of failures and mistakes have been healed forever.

I believe in Christ as my Lord. He rose from the dead and reigns as my victorious conqueror over death. He liberates me from the fear of death and all lesser fears. Now I can live with freedom and joy.

I believe in Christ as indwelling power. He has promised that He will abide in me and I in Him. I invite Him to live in my mind, to think His thoughts through me, to take charge of my will, to guide me to do His will, and to control my emotions to love through me.

I accept the awesome wonder that I am an Easter miracle. By grace, I have been resurrected from the graves of self-centeredness, worry, and anxiety—to live for others. Therefore, I commit my whole life to Christ and will seek to become His faithful and obedient disciple in all my relationships and responsibilities.

For me to live is Christ! I am truly alive, now and forever. Hallelujah and amen.

Chapter Eleven

STOP THE EPIDEMIC!

```
PRESCRIPTION 11:
Commit yourself to motivating people with love
rather than manipulating them with fear.
```

D o you ever get frustrated with people?

Who doesn't?

Getting people to do what we want, when we want it, and how we want it, can be very frustrating.

Trying to change people is even more exasperating, especially when we think we know what's best for them. The things they do and say can infuriate us. And when we see them hurting themselves and others, we want to step in and straighten them out.

Often our impatience reaches a boiling point. It's then that we are tempted to manipulate them with fear. We threaten them with the withdrawal of affection or approval. The law of the jungle—retaliation—becomes our method for getting what we want. Soon we are issuing an ultimatum: "If you don't, I won't!" It's evidence that we've failed to motivate people with love.

To be free of fear, we have to stop using it to get things to go our way. When we rely on fear to coerce people, fear grows in us. The more fear we create in others, the more it tightens its stranglehold on us. That's why I have included this next vital prescription for fearless living: *Commit your-self to motivating people with love rather than manipulating them with fear.*

We need to admit that we all manipulate with fear at times. Then we will be ready to consider how to become dynamic motivators with love.

To better understand how this works, you may find it helpful to picture in your mind's eye the people who frustrate you. Think of those you'd like to change, most of all. Chances are, they are the people closest to you, in your family, among your friends, or at your place of work. In fact, the closer people are to us, the greater our frustration over not being able to get them to march to the drumbeat of our desires.

REALMS OF MANIPULATION

Manipulation with fear often happens in marriage. Many people spend a lifetime trying to transform their mates. Our spouses' habits, personality quirks, attitudes—along with bigger things such as values and beliefs—can distress us. The "for better or for worse" phrase of the marriage vow becomes difficult to keep. Generally, the better we know our mates, the more the "worse" becomes the target of our reformation efforts.

Manipulation with fear is subtle at first. We call it bartering or negotiation. When that fails, many husbands or wives draw a hard line and say, "Do what I want or don't expect me to do what you want!" Sex often becomes a powerful ploy: "If you persist in doing what I've asked you to change, don't come to bed expecting any affection from me!"

But sex is not the only trump card. As soon as we discover what's really important to our mates, we have power. The possibility of withholding whatever that is becomes a manipulative device. And the ultimate manipulation with fear in marriage is, "If you don't change your ways, I'm going to leave!" And the countermanipulation, "Don't bother. If anyone is going to leave, I'll be the first!"

Manipulation with fear is also used to get children to measure up.

Raising a family can be frustrating. We want our kids to reach their full potential. That's usually defined in our own wishes and standards. Sometimes our kids imitate the worst in us and deny our best. We are alarmed by the first and infuriated by the second. And so, the weary task of reminding, scolding, cajoling, and urging goes on through the growing years. We barter privileges for performance. When that doesn't work, parents of teenagers often use fear of punishment or even teeter on the brink of disaster with, "Do it our way or get out!"

Fortunately, in most families, manipulation with fear does not go that far. However, many people reach adulthood having been kept in line with less blatant threats. The tragedy is that most of them repeat the parental pattern of using fear to get others to perform. The lesson has been learned—all too well. They've watched parents manipulate each other and have felt manipulated by fear themselves.

Manipulating with fear can also invade friendships. We all have some friends we'd like to shape up. We get impatient with their priorities or the way they treat others. We get angry when we can't get them to do what *we* think is best for them. Our attitude becomes, "Play the game my way, or I won't play at all." Of course we seldom express it with that crassness; we're just "busy" when they call, or we draw a social circle and exclude them.

Then there's the employment arena. At work, manipulation often crowds out more positive motivation. If we have people working for us, we face the constant challenge of defining goals, clarifying expectations, and inspiring excellence. Working for others isn't a "bed of roses" either, especially if we think we could do their jobs better. But even if we're not bucking for their jobs, getting them to conform to our specifications can give us sleepless nights, if not high blood pressure. "If only they would do things my way!" we mutter.

Some managers use the threat of firing people who don't perform to keep some workers on their toes. But employees have long known the corrosive force of uncooperative and divisive attitudes in the workplace, the undermining power of betrayal in going over a boss's head with a juicy slice of confidential information about his or her ineptness.

The power struggle goes on, and beneath the surface lies manipulation, manipulation that is only possible because of fear.

A Personal Inventory

Pause for a moment and consider ways you have felt manipulated by fear in the realms of marriage, family, friendships, or work. Perhaps the manipulation was not communicated by a direct confrontation, but it was there nonetheless. Unless I miss my guess, it's happened to you. You have felt victimized and pushed around with threats, however veiled they may have been.

Now, I turn to a personal question. Can you identify any relationship in which you are a manipulator rather than a motivator? Strange as it may seem, even when we know how much we abhor being manipulated by fear, we still use it to get others to be who or do what we want, often with the best intentions.

Using Scare Tactics

Recently Larry talked to me about a man he wanted to help. His frustration was at the explosion point. "How do you intend to change this man?" I asked. His reply was one we've all been tempted to express at times. He said, "I'm going to scare the 'hell' out of him and put the fear of God into him!"

Having tried that a few times in my own efforts to help people, I was quick to caution my friend that it wouldn't work. "You can frighten the man, but I doubt whether scaring him will change the 'hell' he's living in, and threatening him with God's judgment will not give him the power to be different. Why not try to put the love of God into him by sharing how God's love has helped you to change? Tell me, how has God helped you?"

My friend's stern, judgmental attitude softened. He could remember two big changes in his life. One was when his doctor told him he was going to have a heart attack unless he changed his lifestyle and lost fifty pounds.

"Did the doctor try to scare the 'hell' out of you?" I asked.

"No," the man responded. "He had been my confidant and trusted adviser for years, and he gave me the prognosis with great empathy and concern."

"Then, how did you lose all the weight?" I queried.

He told me about meeting with a group of church people who encouraged each other to lose weight. He said they were his "cheering section." It was encouragement and love—not fear—that had given my friend victory in his battle to change his eating habits.

The other big change in Larry's life had come in his marriage. One day a few years ago, his wife honestly confessed that she was really hurting in their marriage. "How about her?" I asked. "Did she scare the 'hell' out of you?"

My friend smiled knowingly, indicating that he was getting the point. "Not at all," he said reflectively. "In fact, it was her willingness to admit her part in our problems that opened me up to getting help together. And now we've got a better marriage."

The brief review of how changes had taken place in his own life drained out the anger he was feeling and gave him a desire to encourage the man he had wanted to blast.

Strange, isn't it, how easily we forget how people motivated us with love and fall back on manipulating others with fear?

Another friend of mine has faced how he manipulated his wife to get what he wanted. He now realizes how much fear has dominated his life and relationships.

A few weeks ago he told me, "My motto for people has always been, 'If you screw up, you're history.' With that I could usually keep people in line.

I never felt close to anyone, but most of the time I got what I demanded. What I didn't want was a wife who was frightened of me, but that's exactly what happened. Talk about screwing up! I almost crushed a lovely person!"

GETTING WHAT WE DON'T WANT

It's true! When we use fear to get what we want, we end up with what we don't want—acquiescence, compliance, and a lot of pent-up anger in the people we most want to motivate.

Think of people you've frightened into doing what you want. Remember the panic in their eyes, the jittery nervousness while trying to please you, the mistakes they made under your pressure.

Recall the tenseness you felt trying to maintain the image of perfection while pressuring others to accomplish what you wanted. Reflect on how strained the relationship became.

Most of all, grapple with what happened to your feelings about those people. Chances are, you lost your respect for them. It's difficult to admire people you can push around.

And yet, there are times when we can't help seeing that what people are doing is wrong, and wanting to change them. Even if we give up our idea that we have either the right or the power to change people, we still long to help them. Especially if their actions and attitudes are making them ineffective, isolated, and unhappy.

The only way to help people change is to motivate them with love. That sounds great, but how do we do it? How do we become motivators? Where can we get guidance in helping other people reach their full potential as Christians?

THE CHRISTIAN MOTIVATOR'S GUIDE

The best guide for motivating people I've ever found was written by the apostle Paul. In Romans 12:9-21 Paul gives us the qualifications for authentic Christian motivation. Those qualifications provide us with an incisive inventory of our own motivational skills. As we move through them, we will want to visualize the faces of the people we want to help. To what extent have we communicated these basic qualities?

Be Sure Love Is Your Incentive

The absolutely essential quality of an authentic motivator is love. "Let love be without hypocrisy," Paul says in verse nine. The kind of love he's talking about is the giving, forgiving, unqualified love he has received from Christ. We can't pretend to have that depth of love; it flows as a result of a profound relationship with the Lord.

In reality, *Christ is the master motivator.* It is from Him and how He has worked in our lives that we learn how to motivate and inspire others. He loved us when we least deserved it, and our resistance or rebellion did not dissuade His persistence in loving us.

Christ was more interested in our future than our past. He knew that the things we did were because of the kind of people we were inside. We couldn't change our actions until we were transformed. And our transformation didn't take place until we knew Christ loved us.

The important thing for us to remember is that we can't change anyone. Only Christ can do that. Instead, our function is to be so filled with Christ's love that we love with the power of His love. Notice that I didn't say "copy" His love. That's what Paul meant when he spoke of hypocritical love. A hypocrite is someone who is playing a part, pretending to be what he or she isn't. We are hypocritical lovers of people when we think that, on our own strength, we can imitate Christ's love. That's not our calling; we're simply riverbeds for the flow of His love.

Christ's love must transform our thinking about the person we want to motivate. He wants to help us see him or her as a forgiven, cherished person of ultimate value. Then He wants to help us envision that person's full potential, so we can claim the miracle of change He alone can perform. Once that's clearly implanted in our thinking, what we say to the person and how we relate to him or her will follow naturally. Now comes the hard question. Do the people we'd like to motivate know how much we love them just as they are and that our love is not something we've manufactured but flows from Christ Himself?

But, we object, *if we love people as they are, isn't there a danger that our acceptance will come across as approval of the very things they need to change?* Paul anticipated that question. In the same breath that he challenges us to love without hypocrisy, he says, "Abhor what is evil. Cling to what is good" (Rom 12:9).

We are called to unswerving moral purity in our own lives, but Paul emphasizes that at the same time we must care for those who fail. Like Christ, and with His power, we must hate sin and love sinners. Effective motivators must do both. To help influence other people, our attitudes and words must give them a vivid picture of what it means to live the abundant life in Christ to the fullest without feeling condemned.

Paul wrote that we are to cling to the good. The Greek word for *cling* means "join fast," "glue," "cement," "make one." A positive commitment to live the Ten Commandments plus a vigorous dedication to Christ-centered ethics is the best possible defense against evil. Our faith should be much more than a rules-oriented religion used as a basis for self-righteousness and judgment of others. Instead, it should be a magnetic example to others of the freedom and joy of a Christ-filled and empowered life.

To become attractive witnesses to the Good News of Jesus Christ, we must mirror God's grace. Ask yourself: "Am I living the quality of life I want to motivate in others? Does my love for them, in spite of what they do or say, make my witness dramatically irresistible?" Of course, people need to know where we stand. But they also need to know that we are committed to stand with them in their struggles.

Our love must be expressed in unfailing friendship. Being an understanding and caring friend may very well be our most Christlike act.

Friendship has become a lightweight word in our time. Not so in the Scriptures. It was the highest affirmation of Abraham that he was called a friend of God. Jesus ushered His disciples into a sublime level of intimacy when He said, "No longer do I call you servants, for a servant does not know what his master is doing; but I have called you friends" (Jn 15:15). And to be Christ's friend means befriending others.

Paul tells us the winsome way that this is to be communicated. "Be kindly affectionate to one another with brotherly love, in honor giving preference to one another, not lagging in diligence, fervent in spirit, serving the Lord" (Rom 12:10-11). The last phrase puts befriending those we want to motivate on a dynamic level. Have you ever thought of service to the Lord in terms of being a friend to others?

Notice that Paul lists very specific ways to express that friendship. We must be kind in communicating real affection to the people we want to help. That means telling people how important they are to us, how much we value them, and how fervently we believe in them and their potential.

We must treat them as brothers or sisters who long for the Lord's best in their lives. We must give them time, honoring them as individuals by listening and caring about their needs.

We must be available, quick to respond to their call for help without hesitation, "Not lagging in diligence" (Rom 12:11). The word Paul uses that is translated as *lagging* means "slow" or "poky." Night or day we are to be on call as truly reliable friends of those we are seeking to help and inspire.

Is this too much to ask? Not if we think of the people we're trying to help in the context of serving the Lord. That carries the impact of Jesus' words, "Inasmuch as you did it to one of the least of these My brethren, you did it to Me" (Mt 25:40).

The thought that Christ may come to us in the very people who sometimes frustrate us the most—in the people we want to change—fills us with awe. How we respond to them is really our response to Christ. But the liberating assurance is that God will give us the love we need to motivate people.

Pray for the People You Want to Motivate

The second great quality of an effective motivator is faithfulness in intercessory prayer. We need to spend more time talking to the Lord about a person we want to help than we spend talking to him or her! As Paul puts it in Romans 12:12: "Rejoicing in hope, patient in tribulation, continuing steadfastly in prayer."

Steadfast, consistent, prolonged prayer gives us both hope and patience. Praying for people helps us focus on what the Lord wants for them rather than on our ideas of what they should do or who they should be. Intercessory prayer is not for the purpose of getting the Lord to accomplish our vision for people. Rather, we must allow Him to show us what He wants to do in people's lives.

Often my frustration over people has driven me to prayer for them. I usually begin by telling the Lord *my* agenda for them. Not surprisingly, that never works. But when I commit people to Him and ask for His vision, what I begin to see is so much greater than my wishes. Then my prayers shift into high gear. I know that what I'm asking for is what the Lord is ready to give. I can rejoice in the hope that in His timing and way, it shall be so.

Not only does prayer clarify our hopes for people, it also gives us patience in the process of trying to help them. We need not be precipitate and resort to using fear tactics. At the same time we know that the Lord is at work in the people for whom we pray.

With infinite wisdom He influences people's thoughts, creating a desire to change. As He works out His purposes, He arranges opportunities and prepares the way for our efforts to encourage people. We can count on Christ to be with us, to love through us, to inspire the right words, and to give us strength when we get discouraged. Our prayers for people will lead us to the next step of being a creative motivator.

Tangibilitate!

You'll not find the word *tangibilitate* in your dictionary. It was coined years ago by Father Divine in Harlem. One of his favorite, often-quoted sayings was, "The trouble in religion is that too many people know how to theorize and don't know how to tangibilitate."

It's not difficult to define the meaning of the word for our ministry of motivation. Do something tangible! We need to ask ourselves: What would communicate understanding and caring for the people we want to help? What can we do to lift some burden, meet some need, or provide some special delight? Paul talks about our "distributing to the needs of saints" and being "given to hospitality" (Rom 12:13). He is asking his readers to meet physical needs and welcome people who are strangers. This is our model for all relationships.

Sometimes it means giving financial help or stepping in to assist in a crisis. More often it will be a sensitive, caring act that helps a person know you are committed to being a lasting friend. That can mean anything from making a phone call to see how a person is doing, giving a meaningful gift, interrupting your schedule to listen, helping with a project, to including a person in the inner circle of your cherished friends at a special event.

A "tangibilitating" motivator is innovative. Rather than asking, "What can I do to help?" we take the time and effort to discover what would mean the most to the other person.

I spent one of the most delightful evenings of my life at a surprise party for a friend named Ed. A group of ten of us got together to express our gratitude to him. After the dinner in his honor, each of us had a chance to tell Ed how much we appreciated him for the countless ways he had expressed profound caring for us through the years. We represented a broad spectrum of backgrounds and professions. Though many of us did not know each other, we soon became friends at the party because of our mutual appreciation for Ed.

The central theme of what we had to say to him was that he had motivated us to dare to be our best. Through the ups and downs of life, Ed had always been an invaluable encourager. Some he had helped with personal crises; others he had given hope in times of deep personal problems at home or work; for others he had been a trusted confidant.

The high point of the evening was when Ed made his response. As part of it he repeated from memory the business and personal phone numbers of all of us. That's not a bit surprising. He calls often to spur us on or help lift the load of some need. Why are his calls always so timely? He prays a lot!

You may be thinking that Ed is probably a clergyman or a doctor. No, he's a very successful lawyer who, in addition to a busy practice that spans the nation, knows that his primary calling as a Christian is to motivate people with God's love.

Be an Affirmer

The fourth quality of a motivator is affirmation. It is the power to bless. Paul continues in his list of attitudinal qualities of a Christian motivator with this challenge: "Bless those who persecute you; bless and do not curse" (Rom 12:14). The word *bless* in Greek is *eulogeo,* meaning "speak well of" or "praise" *(eu* = well, *logos* = a word). If we are to speak well of those people on the fringes of our lives who make things difficult for us, we certainly should be careful to motivate those close to us with love and not manipulate them with fear.

What we say to or about a person has the power to bless or curse. And a lack of blessing is in itself a curse. It locks a person into his or her own present stage of growth. We all need affirmation of our worth as persons and our potential to become more than we are now. Affirmation provides self-esteem and hope for the future. It is not dishonest, fulsome flattery, but rather a communication that we are for people and not against them.

Words of affirmation from others are absolutely necessary to penetrate the layers of our own self-doubt and self-negation. We so easily get down on ourselves and become defensive. When others believe in us and encourage us by the blessing of affirmation, we are able to change and grow.

An affirmer is one who has experienced Christ's ultimate affirmation. In spite of all that we've done and been, He loves us. He came to live and die for us that we might know we are loved and forgiven. And now, as reigning Lord, God With Us, He constantly reassures us that we belong to Him. He will never let us go.

When we know that, we can become affirmers of others even when they frustrate us. What they do cannot keep us from believing in what they can become by Christ's transforming power. Our trust is in what He will do; our only responsibility is to affirm that we love them.

A vital expression of our affirmation is to become involved with people in their times of delight and times of suffering. Continuing in Romans 12, Paul encourages us to "rejoice with those who rejoice, and weep with those who weep" (v. 15). Life is a bittersweet blend of success and failure, joy and sorrow. As genuine affirmers of other people, we must be willing to share not only their mountain-peak experiences but their darkest valleys as well. Doing this leads us naturally to the next crucial aspect of motivation.

Focus the Vision
The central challenge of the Christian motivator is to help people envision what their lives could be like if they committed them to Christ, became filled with His Spirit, and guided by His priorities and goals for them. Our task is not to bend people to our will or our ideas of what might be best for them. Instead, we must ask penetrating questions that press them to evaluate where they are going in their lives, what kind of people they want to become, and what kind of relationships they want to have. Our challenge is to help put people in touch with the Master.

Paul further encourages us to "be of the same mind toward one another" (v. 16). That really means "thinking the same thing" or "thinking together." This means blending action and feelings. What we think about Christ and His will for us directly controls what we become. Therefore, truly creative motivators will inspire other people to allow Christ to repattern their minds in conformity with His will and purpose.

The secret of transforming human personality is receiving the mind of Christ. "Let this mind be in you which was also in Christ Jesus," Paul encouraged his readers in Philippians 2:5. And to the Corinthian Christians he wrote, "For 'who has known the mind of the Lord that he may instruct Him?' But we have the mind of Christ" (1 Cor 2:16). The mind of Christ is the motivating power for reorienting our thinking, reforming our wills, and remolding our feelings.

Too few Christians have discovered the gift of Christ's indwelling mind. That's why our thinking about life is often so confused, our values and priorities so inconsistent with His, and our personalities so far from being like His. Any effort to motivate people to change or grow that skims over the deepest need we all have—to receive the mind of Christ—is surface meddling that brings no lasting results.

Often, problems and crises provide opportunities to talk with people about the direction and goals of their lives. The presence of conflict in our relationships should awaken us to the kinds of things we may be doing that turn people off and stand in the way of their response to the Lord.

At times, however, there *is* a need for us to be graciously confrontive. The word *confront* has taken on some harsh baggage in our society. That's unfortunate because it really means "have face-to-face communication."

Any confrontation must always be preceded by caring and companionship. Only then can we share with people how Christ works in our lives to deal with problems or challenges similar to theirs. Then they can feel free to ask themselves hard questions about their lives. And it's only then that they will come to their own conclusions about their needs, and we can lovingly share our hope and vision for them.

Be Vulnerable
In the dynamic process of motivating people, vulnerability about our own needs and discoveries is essential. Only a person who is changing can help others to change. No one has it all together. Anyone who tries to pretend that he or she does have it all together cannot be an effective motivator.

Vulnerability makes us approachable. When we feel free to share what the Lord is doing with the raw material of our imperfect personalities, people are drawn to us and feel free to share their lives with us. Because the Lord is never finished with us, there's always a next step of growth we need to take.

For example, in this chapter I've been trying to share some of the most liberating discoveries I've made about being a Christ-empowered motivator. With all my mind and heart, I believe that motivating people with love is the only alternative to manipulating them with fear.

And yet, living what I've written is one of the greatest challenges of my life. I'm constantly tempted to bypass the steps of motivation by love based on Paul's words in Romans 12.

Sometimes, under the pressure of a busy schedule, I neglect my personal relationships with the very people I want to help. Then I wonder why my suggestions and advice are not well received. At such times, though, the Lord gently reminds me that my relationships with people I want to motivate must always be kept in good repair.

From this you can see that you and I are fellow strugglers in attempting to live without fear.

A friend who had worked with and for me as a fellow pastor once introduced me to an audience as an impatient man with a vision. I was shocked. I like to think of myself as a patient person. Later my friend told me that he had intended to communicate that I express the urgency to press on in the renewal of the church and the preparation and training of Christians for ministry in the world.

The truth is, I am an impatient person, in some less noble ways than my friend explained. I get impatient with the institutional process. I often want things done yesterday. And I tire of religious people who miss the adventure of exhilarating discipleship.

Usually, my impatience is caused by inner impatience with myself. That's when I must take an extra measure of time in my own prayers to receive fresh grace. The Lord is faithful: He reminds me of how patient He has had to be with me over the years. In these times of prayer, I am refreshed and renewed to be a loving and vulnerable motivator of people.

Paul put it directly when he wrote, "Do not set your mind on high things, but associate with the humble. Do not be wise in your own opinion" (Rom 12:16). The apostle is not suggesting we give up our goals, but he is cautioning us about a false security in our own accomplishments. Instead, we must "associate with the humble." The Greek actually means "be carried away with lowly things." In other words, we are to remember what the Lord has done for us and still needs to accomplish in us.

Believe me, the Lord has a way of knocking down our arrogant perfectionism by showing us who we really are. At such moments we become well aware that the kind of growth we are trying to inspire in others is also needed in our own lives. This leads us to the last quality of a motivator.

Never Give Up

A Christ-inspired motivator never gives up. Knowing that the Master will never give up on us, we are not given the luxury of giving up on other people. Paul concludes his list of admonitions for the Christian communicator with three negative challenges that convey a very positive impact.

First, *don't retaliate.* "Repay no one evil for evil. Have regard for good things in the sight of all men. If it is possible, as much as depends on you, live peaceably with all men" (Rom 12:17-18). For the Christian motivator, this simply means that we are not to reject people who do not respond to our overtures of love. We can't write people off as long as the Lord has another chapter to write in their lives. We must keep on praying, caring, and being available.

To "live peaceably," means to keep the relationship going, maintaining channels of communication. Peace implies a harmonious relationship. For me, that requires both timing and long-haul persistence. It's easy to win a battle by telling people how bad they are and lose the war of helping them claim how great they can be in Christ.

Second, *don't play God.* Paul says, "Beloved, do not avenge yourselves, but rather give place to wrath; for it is written, '"Vengeance is Mine, I will repay," says the Lord'" (Rom 12:19). This brings us full circle to where we began in our discussion of using fear to get what we want from people. When we threaten to punish or actually take judgment into our own hands, we not only lose our effectiveness to influence them positively, we also provoke anger that distracts people from coming to grips with what God wants to do in their lives.

I think that's what Paul has in mind when he quotes Proverbs 25: 21-22:

> Therefore, if your enemy hungers, feed him;
> If he thirsts, give him a drink;
> For in so doing you will heap coals of fire on his head.
>
> ROMANS 12:20

Coals of fire symbolize the judgment, purification, and cleansing of God.

How does giving food and drink to our enemy do that? It simply dissipates their anger toward us and forces them to deal with God. Our persistence in personal and practical caring for people when they seem to deserve it the least can create a desire to know the Source of our unconquerable love for them.

"Coals of fire" may also mean a burning conviction. Other Semitic proverbs refer to "coals in the heart" and "fire in the liver" as a flaming passion. In Isaiah 6:1-8 it was a coal of fire from the altar that renewed Isaiah's vision and hope. In the New Testament fire is a key metaphor for the Holy Spirit. We are not far from that key meaning when we claim that our persistent love will provide the spark that sets the fire of the Lord burning in another person.

Third, *don't give in to discouragement.* Paul continues, "Do not be overcome by evil, but overcome evil with good" (Rom 12:21). Discouragement is Satan's most powerful weapon. His five most debilitating words are "It won't make any difference." Discouragement is really a build-up of fear.

Far from being the problem of a few depressed people, discouragement lurks beneath the surface in most people. They need to know that we really believe the five most powerful words of a motivator, "Love makes all the difference!"

Each time we refuse to use fear to manipulate others, we overcome evil with good. Satan's program of trying to overcome good with fear is given one more defeat. Remember, we're counterculture Christians called to reverse the epidemic of fear in our world. The Lord is at work through us. Daily He encourages us with signs of progress. We don't have to rely on fear.

Don't underestimate the power of your ministry of motivation. It's why we were born and reborn. We don't have to be conduits of fear. We can be channels of love.

Chapter Twelve

BLESSED ASSURANCE

PRESCRIPTION 12:
*Give up the vague idea that, given time, things work
out. Boldly face the future unafraid with the sure
confidence that God will work all things for
your ultimate good and His glory.*

"We did the best we could," the surgeon told Stan's family. We got most of the malignancy, but as soon as Stan can take it, we're going to have to go back in after the rest of the tumor."

I listened intently to the surgeon's report as I sat with Stan's family in a hospital waiting room after the first of several operations that saved his life.

The surgeon's words express my feelings as I begin this final chapter. We've been inside our minds and hearts, cutting away at the malignancy of fear that robs us of the joy of living. Now we must cut even more as we look ahead into the future.

Our fear of the future is not just caused by the uncertainty about tomorrow. It goes much deeper than that. A profound pessimism lurks inside most people. It's prompted by disappointment with a heresy I see among Christian believers.

Simply stated, this heresy is expressed in a trite maxim: "Given time, everything works out." I don't believe that. Nor do I believe that "time heals all wounds." This is little more than a sophisticated, but still blind, trust in fate. All too often we're guilty of saying to ourselves and others, "Don't worry, things have a way of working out." But sometimes things don't work out.

Many Christians who claim an assurance of heaven still have a deep fear about what's going to happen to them between now and the time of their physical death. Some feel victimized by seemingly uncontrollable events. We thank God for the good things that happen, but what about the pain and difficulties? When we've had more than our share of problems, we fear that the future will simply become an endurance contest.

A KEY VERSE

Karla felt that way. "I feel utterly defenseless," she said. "Up to this point I've felt that if I were patient, things would work out for the best. Now I'm at the end of my patience." Do you ever feel that way? Do you look back over the deep troublesome valleys of your life and wonder, "Will the future hold anything more?" Then we take an extra large dose of the bromide that somehow things will work out. "Just hang in there," we urge ourselves. "Everything works out for those who wait. You've gotta believe the Bible; all things work together for good."

That sounds like good advice, doesn't it? Wrong! It's based on the wording of Romans 8:28 as it was translated in 1611 for the *King James Version* of the Bible. Many of us memorized that verse this way, "And we know that all things work together for good to them that love God, to them who are the called according to his purpose."

This wording places the emphasis on things working out in the lives of people who love God. That gave rise to this idea that, given enough time, things will work out. And the next step was the development of the vague trust in eventuality rather than in God.

This ambiguous hope for the future, however, becomes clearer when we understand that in the original Greek the order of the words in this verse puts the meaning in true perspective and gives us a cure for our fear of the future. "For we know that to those who love God, in all things God works together for good to those who are called according to His purpose" (my translation).

Things don't work out. God works out things! That truth not only contradicts the current heresy but fills us with courage and expectancy for the rest of our lives on earth. It also paves the way for our twelfth and final prescription for living without fear: *Give up the vague idea that, given time, things work out. Boldly face the future unafraid with the sure confidence that God will work all things for your ultimate good and His glory.*

GOD IS OUR FUTURE

Let's begin where Paul did in his words of assurance for the Christians in Rome. God is our future. He created us to receive and return His love. In Christ, He reconciled us to Himself so that we could know and love Him. We couldn't do that on our own.

Saint Augustine had this truth in mind when he prayed, Lord, "give what You ask and ask what You will." When Christ takes up residence in our minds and hearts, He loves the Father through us. He gives us the freedom to claim His gift of family likeness with Him.

We have been chosen by God and called to live with trusting confidence in His goodness. The future is a gift in which Christ accomplishes His purpose in and through us. What is God's purpose? It is to make us like His Son!

When we commit ourselves to becoming like Christ, we begin the process of liberation from fear of the future. Everything else must be secondary. No person, plan, or program can be placed ahead of this goal. When being like Christ becomes our sole purpose in life, we become the special focus of the Father's fear-dispelling love. By grace alone, we can participate in the love between the Father and the Son. Christ in us gives us the power to truly love the Father. That love qualifies us to be counted among the people Paul calls "those who love God."

How God Works

Just as God arranged circumstances to bring us to the place of willingness to receive Christ, so, too, He uses all of life to help us grow in Christ. He entrusts management of that growth to His Son.

Christ is with us watching over all that happens to us. He goes before us to guide us each step into the future. He is beside us as our Companion and Friend, and He is behind us to gently prod us when we lag behind with caution and reluctance. Most of all, Christ is in our minds to help us understand the purpose of what happens to and around us. Moment by moment, He shows us that He is using the events of life to strengthen in us the fiber of His nature and character.

I don't think we have to wait until the end of our lives to understand why we have encountered life's dark threads as well as the threads of gold and silver. If we come to the Lord with an open, receptive mind, He will give us exactly the insight we need to understand His deeper purpose. He interprets what happened the day before and inspires us to trust Him for the day ahead. For anything He chooses not to interpret now, He gives us the quiet assurance to wait. I like the way William Cowper expressed this assurance:

> God's purposes will ripen fast,
> Unfolding every hour:
> The bud may have a bitter taste,
> But sweet will be the flower....
> God is His own interpreter,
> And He will make it plain.

Uses Everything

The crucial truth the Lord, our Interpreter, wants to make plain is that He will use everything that happens to us for the accomplishment of His awesome purpose. That's what He impressed on Paul's mind and validated in his experience.

At the end of his third missionary journey, around A.D. 57, Paul could look back and see how the Lord had been orchestrating the events of his life. Nothing had been wasted. The triumphs and the tragedies had been used to mold the clay of his nature into the image of Christ. Paul had known success and failure, victory and defeat, acclaim and rejection.

One thing can account for Paul's resiliency and his confidence for the future. The years had taught him well that, "All things God works together for good to those who are called according to His purpose."

We can't face the future without fear until we are absolutely sure of that truth. Of course we still make mistakes, bring problems on ourselves, and resist the Lord's best for our lives. But there is just no way one can face the future with confidence without the firm hope that the Lord will make the best of our efforts and help us to grow through our failures.

At the same time, it is important we understand that not all of our problems are of our own making. Often we are victims of other people's ineptness or confused motives. Our future is peopled with the full spectrum of proud, selfish, competitive, greedy humankind. Our tomorrows will be invaded by conflict and broken relationships. But we can endure people problems if we know for sure that the Lord will help us, and, if we know that, He will use even the difficulties to deepen our relationship with Him.

Our assurance that He will use all things for our growth and His glory must also extend to the realities of pain, sickness, and death. Through it all, we will need to know that He is both our Healer and our Strength to endure. We will know His miraculous interventions and His patience when we need to wait. Mysteriously, He will use our times of physical weakness to teach us to depend on Him. And when we walk through the valley of the shadow of death, He will be there to lead us all the way to heaven.

Neither the crafty influences of evil nor the calamities of the natural world are beyond the Lord's power to use for our good. He is with us to help us overcome evil and to trust Him through tragedies. Nothing can separate us from Him or His creative purposes for us.

Works Together

Believing that God works all things together for good does not exempt us from difficulties, but it does assure us of exceptional power to handle them. It helps to remember that God does not send trouble to force us to grow. There's already an abundance of trouble in this fallen, rebellious world that refuses to accept His sovereignty. And yet, in spite of humankind's rejection of Him, He rules and overrules to protect, guide, and care for "those who are the called according to His purpose."

The way the Lord "works things together for good" is to block us from getting into some troubles, strengthen us in others, and turn still others into stepping stones. Nothing escapes His loving providence. He is constantly working to increase our joys and strengthen us in our difficulties.

The Greek verb for *works together* also means "works with." The Lord not only works things together with perfect timing for our good; He works with us, helping us understand His purpose. We discover that often it is in life's tight places, troublesome problems, and painful experiences that we have made the longest strides in our growth as people.

That's the confidence that cures fear of the future. We are promised neither a trouble-free future nor one in which *things* will eventually work out. What we are promised is that God will work all things together with creative continuity for our ultimate good. Tomorrow is under His control. We don't have to try to hold back the dawn or flinch at the problems it may bring.

We can rest comfortably with the assurance that God knows what He's doing! He's with us in Christ. And the Master whispers in our hearts, "Don't be anxious about tomorrow. God will take care of your tomorrow too. Live one day at a time" (Mt 6:34, LB).

NEW EVERY MORNING

The conviction that God uses everything and brings His best for us out of the worst that might happen must be reaffirmed every morning. Some great verses to repeat the moment we wake up are found in Lamentations 3:22-24. Start your day with this mind-opener about God:

> His compassions fail not.
> They are new every morning;
> Great is Your faithfulness.
> "The Lord is my portion," says my soul,
> "Therefore I hope in Him!"

I've repeated that daily for years. Beginning the morning that way has helped me to remember that the Lord has enabled me to grow through problems and make my most exciting discoveries while wrestling with difficulties. That's especially helpful when I wake up tense, with a problem I have to face that day weighing heavily on my mind.

I remember one morning, awaking with a big problem on my mind. My stomach was knotted with feelings of fear. Fear gripped my emotions. Then I repeated Jeremiah's affirmation of God's faithfulness. After that, I lay in bed going over what might happen. However bad it might be, I knew from experience that the Lord would use it. So I began to praise Him for what I was going to learn through the problem. Only then did the fear subside. I felt new strength to get up and tackle the problem.

All through the day, as I faced the problem head-on, I kept praying, "Lord, what are You trying to teach me in this? What good do You want to bring out of it?" As it turned out, the Lord not only helped me find a solution to the problem but used what I had been through to help someone else.

That evening, I had dinner with a friend, Jason, who asked me, "What do you do when you awake at four in the morning feeling fearful over what's ahead in the day? I feel like I want to cancel the day, turn off the alarm clock set for six o'clock, pull the covers over my head, and just not get up."

Jason confided that lately he'd had a lot of mornings like that; between four and six had become what he called "worry time." Problems were magnified as he dramatized in his mind all the terrible things that might happen.

I shared with Jason what I'd been through that very day and the fresh experience I'd had of seeing the Lord bring good out of a worrisome problem.

"Jason," I said, "it sounds like we are soul brothers. Why don't we covenant to pray for each other, specifically that we will turn our early morning worry time into praise time? When a problem wakes us up, let's give it to the Lord and spend our time praying about the best He could bring out of it rather than the worst we can imagine. Then let's claim the vision He gives us and thank Him that He will work it all out in His timing and way."

Months later we got together, and he said, "Do you know what? I think the Lord has pulled off an old-fashioned miracle in this crusty ol' Presbyterian. The other day I realized that my feelings of dread about the future are completely gone!"

The secret of Jason's liberation came in recognizing that all his fears were related to secondary things—his family, health, job, and reputation. He needed to focus on God's goal for his life. And when he did that, he became confident that God would work all the secondary concerns together to accomplish that goal.

God's Grand Plan for Our Lives

The only sure way to overcome fear of the future is to make God's "good" our goal. God doesn't work all things together just to set us free from fear. That's a by-product of committing our lives to His plan and submitting to His agenda for fulfilling it.

We've come full circle from where we began: The good for which God works everything together is to make us like Christ. We don't need to fear anything that might happen to us in the future, because we belong to God. He will not allow anything to happen that He will not use for His plan. God never gives up on us or on His purpose for us.

That was Paul's conviction as he neared the end of his life, in prison in Rome. We suspect the message he communicated to Christians in Rome was what he also wrote to the Philippian Christians. Believers in both churches were afraid. They faced opposition, persecution, and discouragement. In response, Paul shared the steadfast confidence he had for himself and for them. "Being confident of this very thing," he wrote in Philippians 1:6, "that He who has begun a good work in you will complete it until the day of Jesus Christ."

The "good work" the Lord had begun in Paul and the early Christians was the same as the "good" for which God was working all things together: the miracle of shaping them into the image of Christ. That's His plan and purpose. What the Lord has begun in us, He will complete. All the resources of heaven and the present ministry of Christ are committed to assure us of victory. Once His "good work" has begun in us, He will use all the outer trials we face to build up our inner person. He provides exactly what we need each day.

Billy Graham discovered this early in his ministry. Just before he began his crusades many years ago in Los Angeles, he attended a conference sponsored by the First Presbyterian Church of Hollywood at Forest Home in the San Bernardino Mountains. Dr. Graham has talked about what that time at Forest Home meant to him as he experienced the Lord's power to press on in full realization of the "good work" that the Lord had begun in him.

During the Forest Home conference Dr. Graham was engaged in a spiritual battle, wrestling with doubts about his faith. One evening he followed a path into the woods. "I made up my mind on that day," he said, "I would either give up what little Christian faith I had or discover a stronger base upon which to stand for Christ." Alone beneath the evening sky, he opened the Bible. This verse leapt out at him: "He who has begun a good work in you will complete it until the day of Jesus Christ." At that moment, Billy Graham surrendered himself to God and the gifts of the Holy Spirit.

"It dawned on me," he said later, "that what faith I had was a gift of God, that His reserves were boundless, that if I would consent to receive, He was ready, willing, and able to keep on giving."

Since then Dr. Graham has of course preached to millions of people, and hundreds of thousands have been converted to Christ through his love-motivated preaching. The "good work" the Lord began has never stopped growing in greater power and effectiveness.

THE FOCUS OF OUR ATTENTION

Fear of the future invades our minds and hearts when we focus on the evil around us and not on Christ and what He is doing to complete God's "good work" in us. Actually the fear we feel is like a bell on a channel buoy. It rings to alert us that we are off course.

I've never known it to fail. When I worry about the future, that's the time the Lord breaks through. By helping me trust Him more, He leads me to a bold new step in experiencing the "character transplant" of Christ's life in me.

Then the truths I've held in a vague way become concrete through my experience, and I can pray for myself the prayer Paul prayed for the Philippian Christians:

And this I pray, that your love may abound still more and more in knowledge and all discernment, that you may approve the things that are excellent, that you may be sincere and without offense ... being filled with the fruits of righteousness which are by Jesus Christ, to the glory and praise of God.

PHILIPPIANS 1:9-11

Note the progression in the prayer. The Lord's overflowing love makes us able to understand and experience His faithfulness and goodness in all that happens to us. The word for *knowledge* that Paul uses is "experienced truth" as opposed to "conceptual ideas." We can be aware of the Lord's presence in spite of the difficulties we encounter.

That motivates us to seek His excellence, the highest potential for our growth in all things. Then we long to cooperate in the continued development of His "good work" in us, and we are sincere about pressing on.

The Greek word for *sincere* means "judged by the sunlight," while its Latin counterpart means "without wax," and is used for a piece of pottery in which the imperfections had not been filled with wax to make the piece look perfect. For us, sincerity means holding our lives up to the light of Christ, being thankful for our growth so far and not trying to cover up our needs. We can be honest and open about our next steps of growth in becoming like Christ. Happily, He is not finished with us: we are not who we were, and, thanks to Him, who we are is only the beginning of what He has planned for us.

CONTAGIOUS FAITH

Paul vividly illustrates from his own life how the Lord can use everything to help us grow and then use us to encourage others who fear the future. "I want you to know, brethren, that the things which happened to me have actually turned out for the furtherance of the gospel" (Phil 1:12). He goes on to explain that his imprisonment gave him opportunities to lead the guards to Christ and gave new boldness to the Christians in Rome.

While Paul was imprisoned, his guards were chained to him. Imagine being chained to the apostle Paul! It has been said that many of the guards had to be relieved of that duty because they were becoming Christians as a result of prolonged contact with Paul. These guards came to realize that, in reality, Paul was bonded to Christ. And that liberating bondage made Paul the most "free" person in history. His faith was contagious. Even in difficult circumstances, the "good work" of the Lord in Paul continued to grow.

ASSURANCE

The same is true for us. Our confidence is not that things work out, but that God works out things!

With that assurance we can retake our prescriptions for living without fear. I've never outgrown my need to review them daily and claim the Lord's power for each bold step. Join me, and together we will experience God's fear-conquering presence.

TWELVE PRESCRIPTIONS FOR LIVING WITHOUT FEAR

1. Your fear is really loneliness for God. Therefore, claim His promise never to leave nor forsake you.

2. Overcome your crippling fears with a creative fear of God expressed in awe and wonder, adoration and faithful obedience. He is the only Person you have to please.

3. Face your fears; retrace them to their source in your heart; displace them by making your heart Christ's home; and erase them with God's perfect love.

4. Let go of hurting memories from the past. Do not anticipate the repetition of past pain; accept forgiveness from the Lord; and forgive everything and everyone from the past—including yourself.

5. What you fear in others, you first fear in yourself. Therefore, in response to God's unqualified acceptance, embrace yourself as worthy of your own affirmation and encouragement.

6. Admit that you are inadequate to meet life's opportunities. You can conquer your fear by becoming a riverbed for the flow of God's guidance, love, and power.

7. You are secure in God's love. Do not surrender your self-worth to the opinions and judgments of others. When you are rejected, do not retaliate; when you are hurt, allow God to heal you. And knowing the pain of rejection, seek to love those who suffer from its anguish.

8. Turn over control of your life to the Lord. Trust His control over what you were never meant to control. Take responsibility for what He has given you to do for His glory and by His power.

9. Confess your fearful imagination and ask the Lord today, through His Spirit, to make your imagination a channel of His vision and not a breeding place for fear.

10. Face your eventual physical death and claim that you are alive eternally. Then you can live abundantly without panic for the rest of your time on earth.

11. Commit yourself to motivating people with love rather than manipulating them with fear.

12. Give up the vague idea that, given time, things work out. Boldly face the future unafraid with the sure confidence that God will work all things for your ultimate good and His glory.

Notes

Chapter 2
Whom Shall I Fear?

1. Betty Cuniberti, "Yuppie Angst—Coping With the Stress of Success," *Los Angeles Times,* 21 November 1986, V-20.

Chapter 5
Have You Hugged Yourself Today?

1. Cited in Steve Brown, "Harry and the Humble Habit," *Christian Life,* October 1986, 30.

Chapter 6
Who Can? The Gift of Inadequacy

1. John Henry Jowett, *Evangel,* 8 March 1976.

Chapter 7
You Think You've Got Enemies?

1. Somerset Maugham, *The Moon and Sixpence* (New York: George H. Doran, 1919).
2. Frank Houghton, *Amy Carmichael of Dohnavar* (Fort Washington, Pa.: Christian Literature Crusade, 1979).
3. Ruth Harms Calkin, *Tell Me Again, Lord, I Forget* (Wheaton, Ill.: Tyndale House, 1986).

Chapter 9
Can You Imagine?

1. Words and music by Paul Baskin. Copyright 1987. Used by permission.

Chapter 10
Death, Where Is Your Sting?

1. I highly recommend Amy Harwell's outstanding book, *When Your Friend Gets Cancer: How You Can Help* (Wheaton, Ill.: Harold Shaw, 1987). She explains what she discovered and how to help others who face cancer.